DISCOVERING ROME
ITALY

The Eternal City

PICTORIAL SEARIES

Presented by

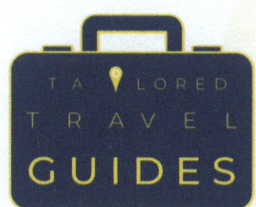

Discover your journey!

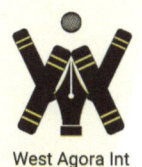

a WEST AGORA INT S.R.L. Brand
www.tailoredtravelguides.com
Edited by WEST AGORA INT S.R.L.
WEST AGORA INT S.R.L. All Rights Reserved
Copyright © WEST AGORA INT S.R.L., 2023

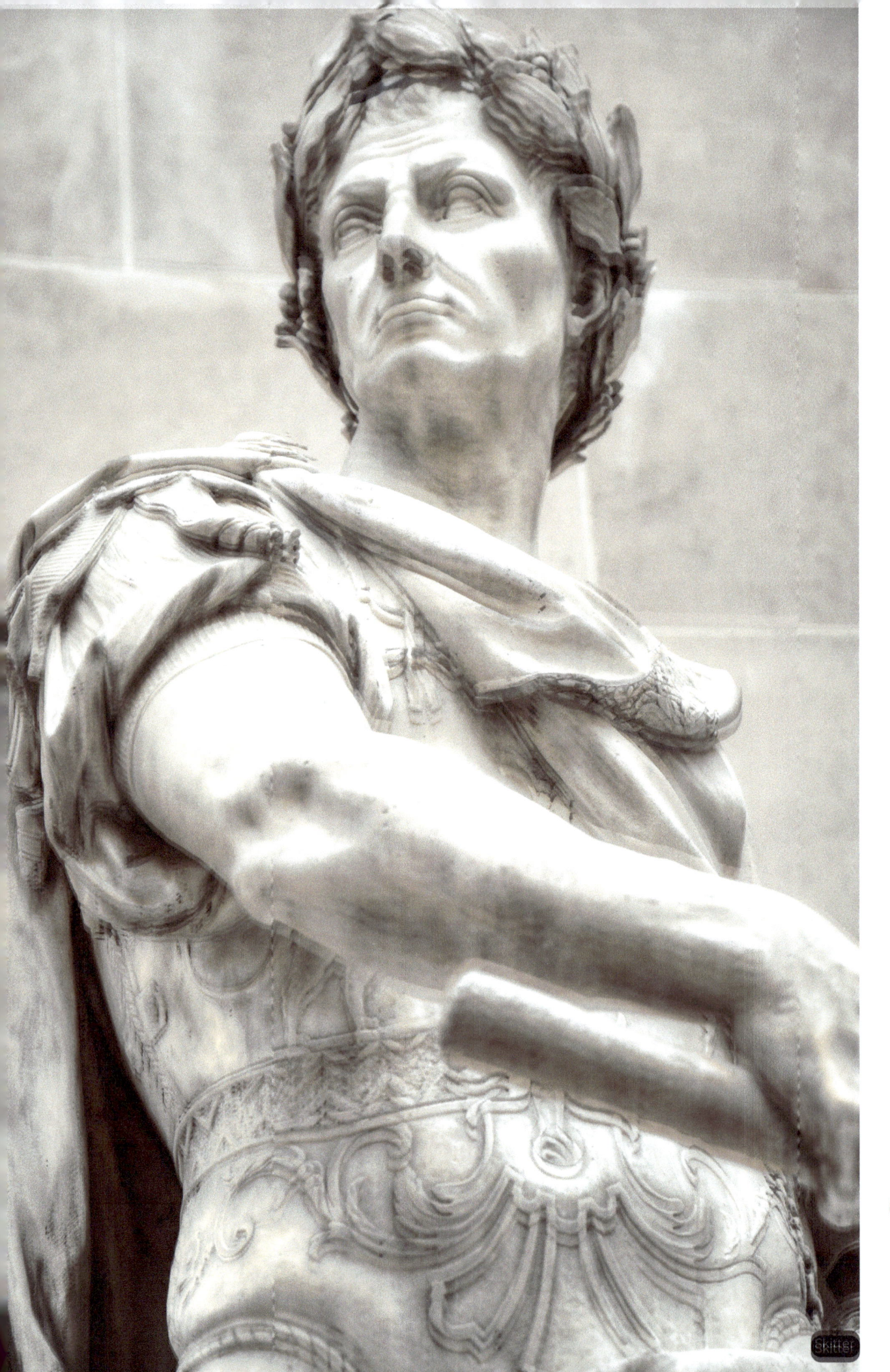

Julius Caesare marble statue

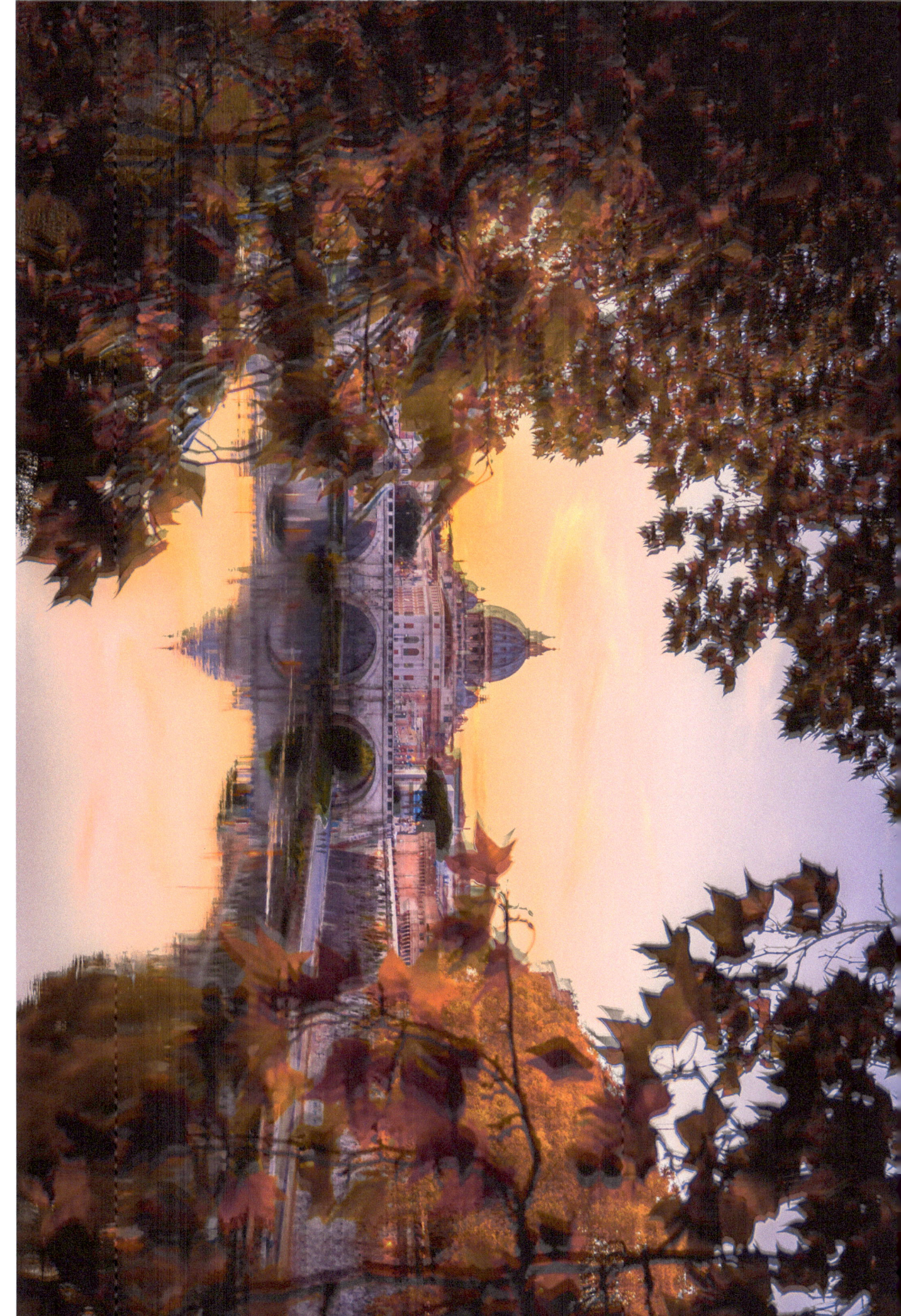

View over St. Peter's Basilica

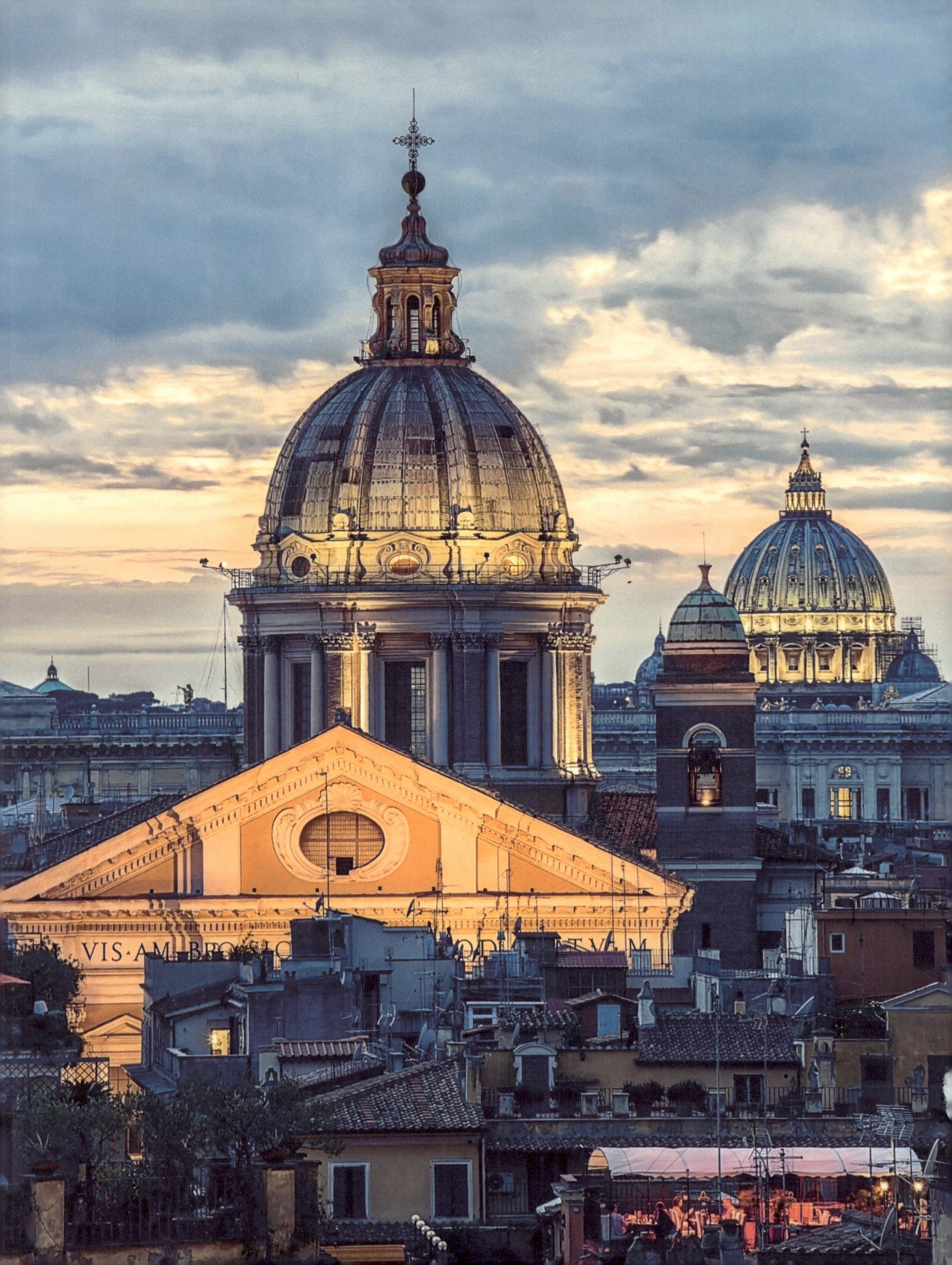

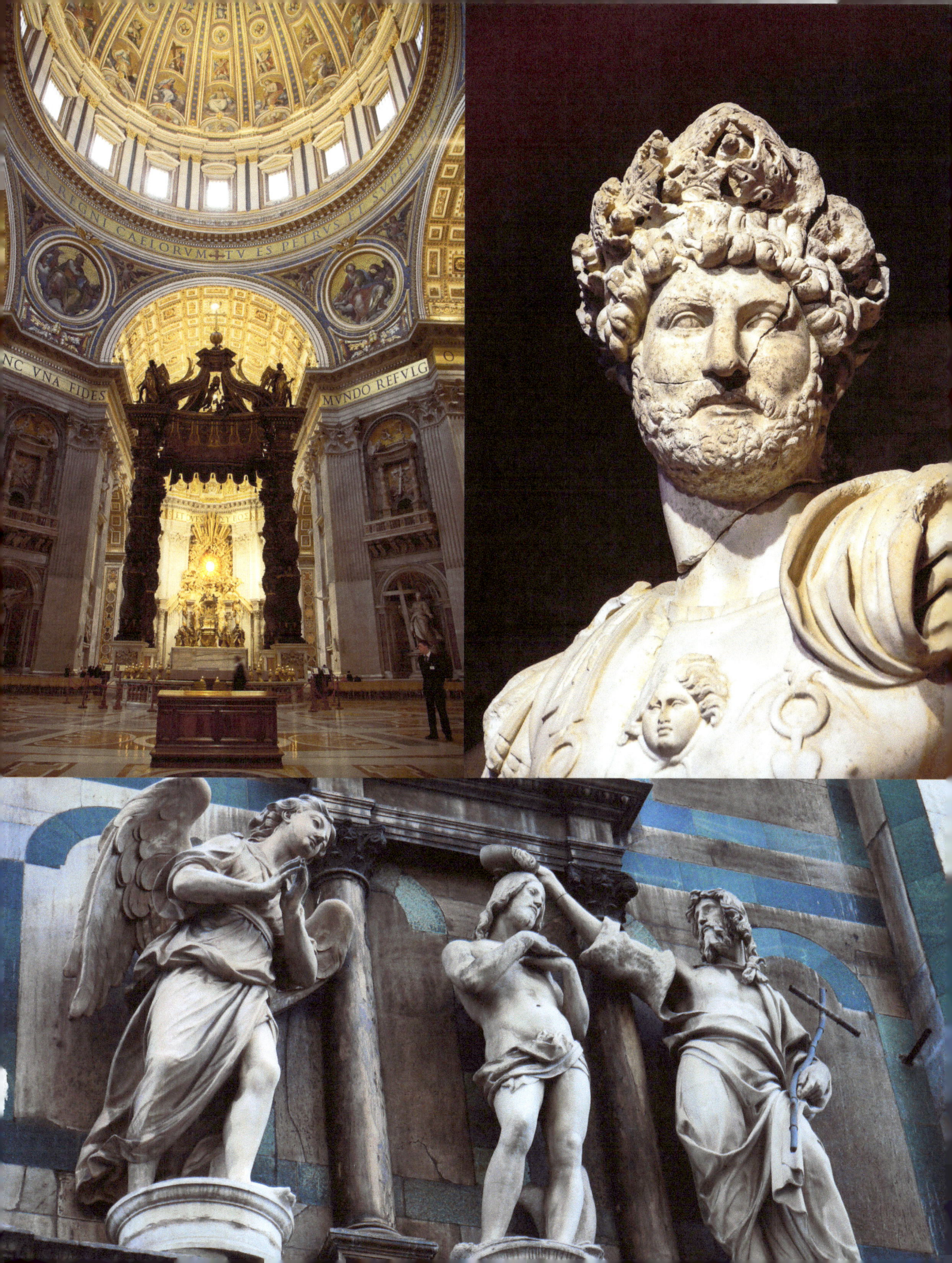

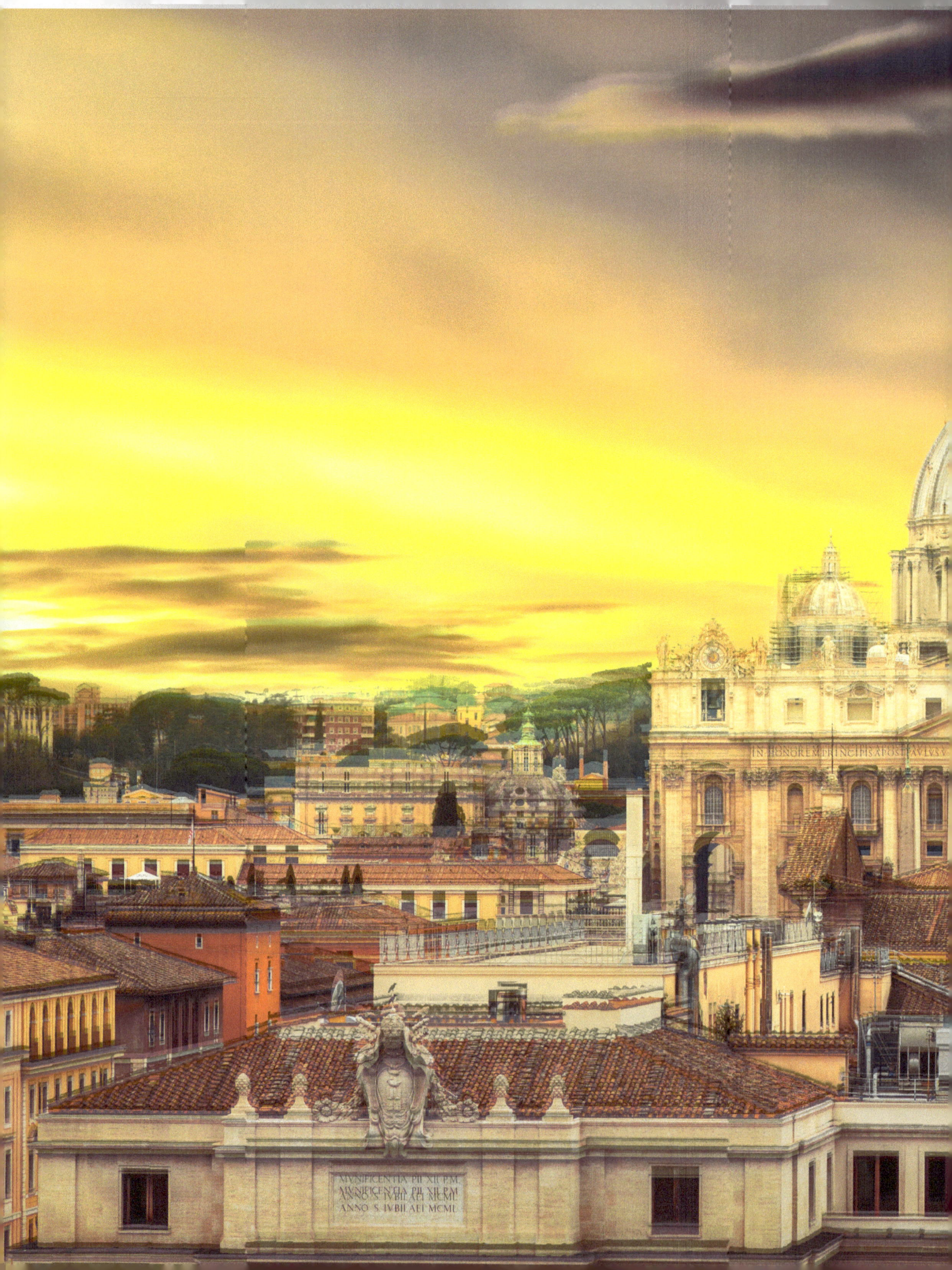

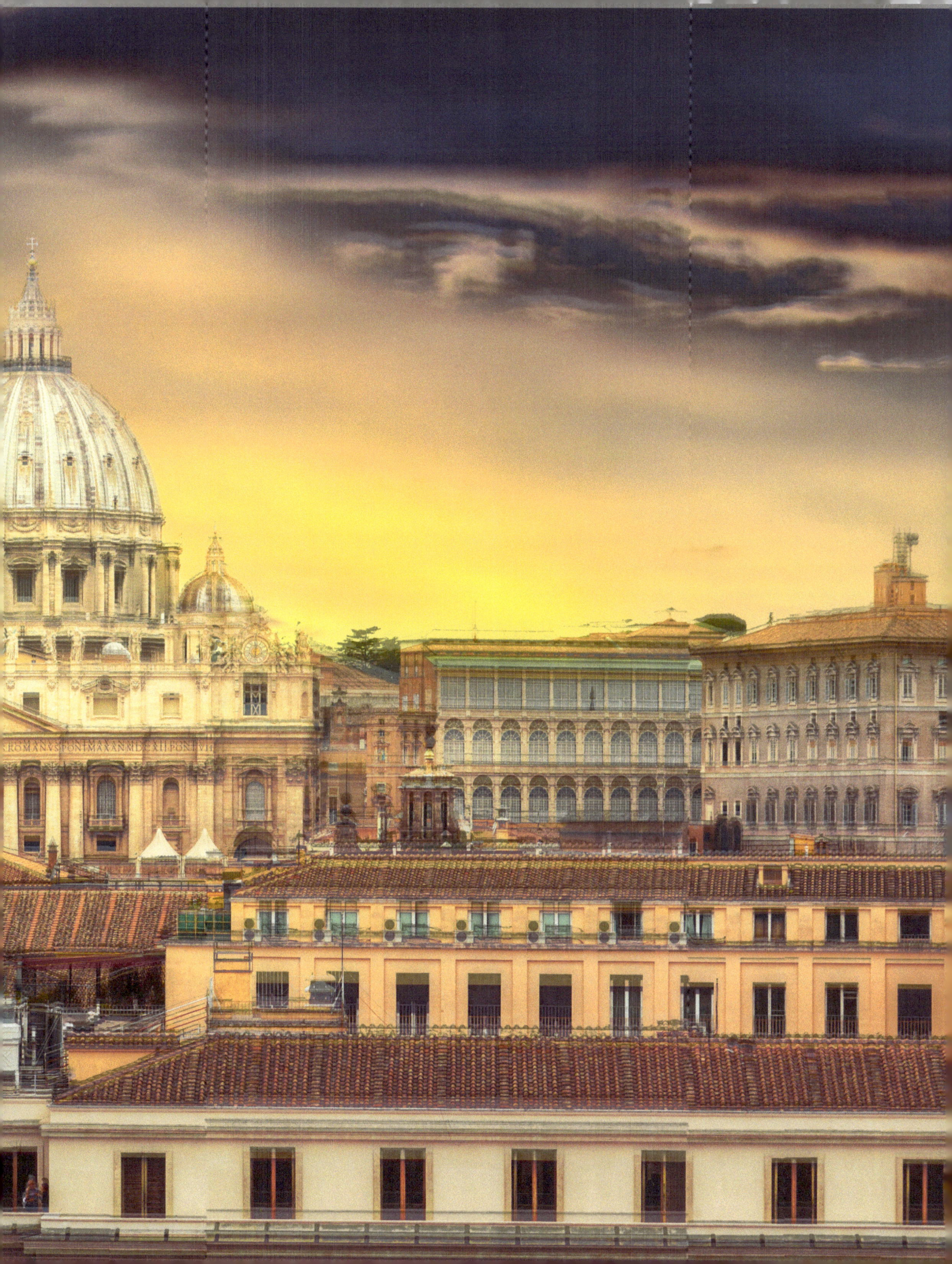

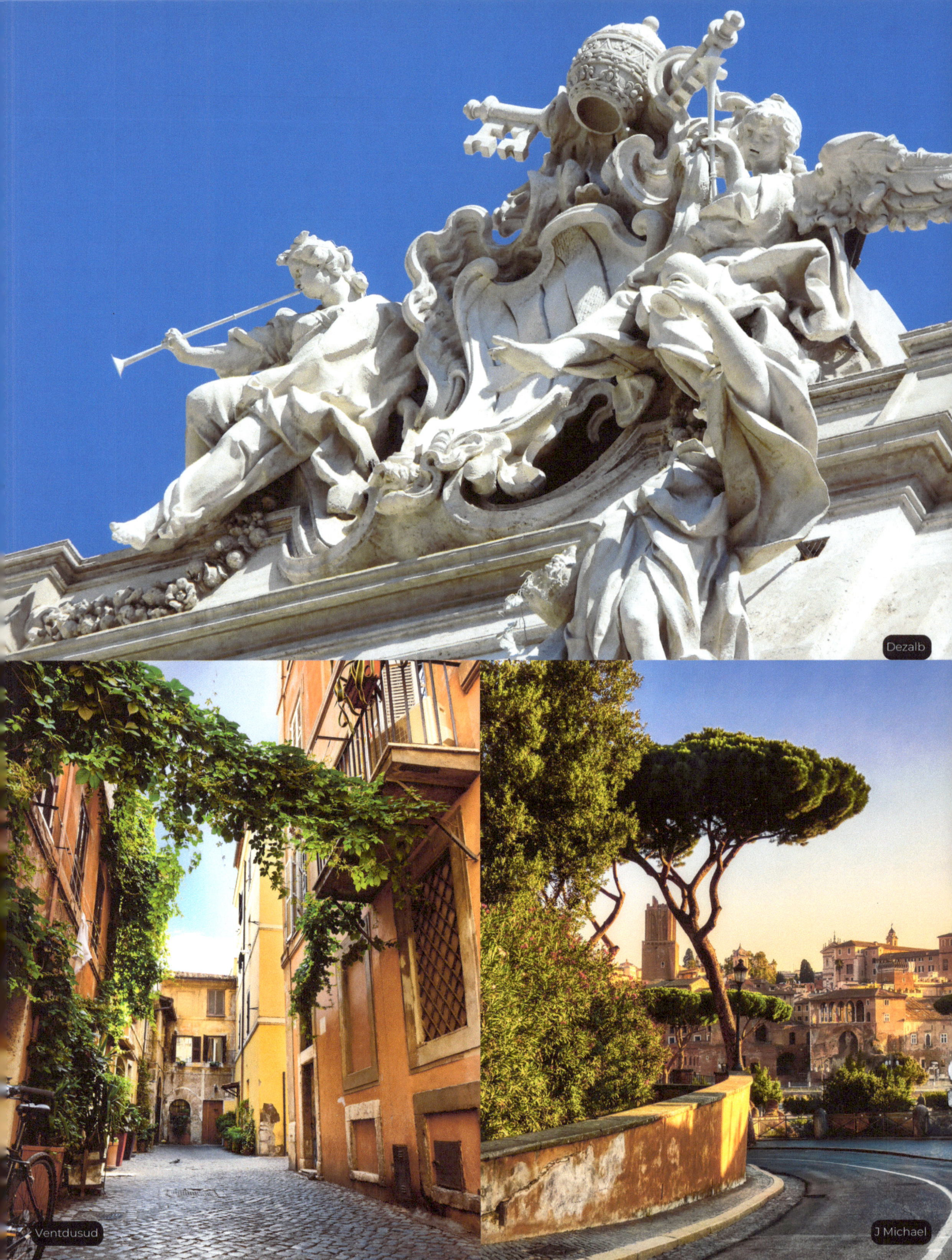

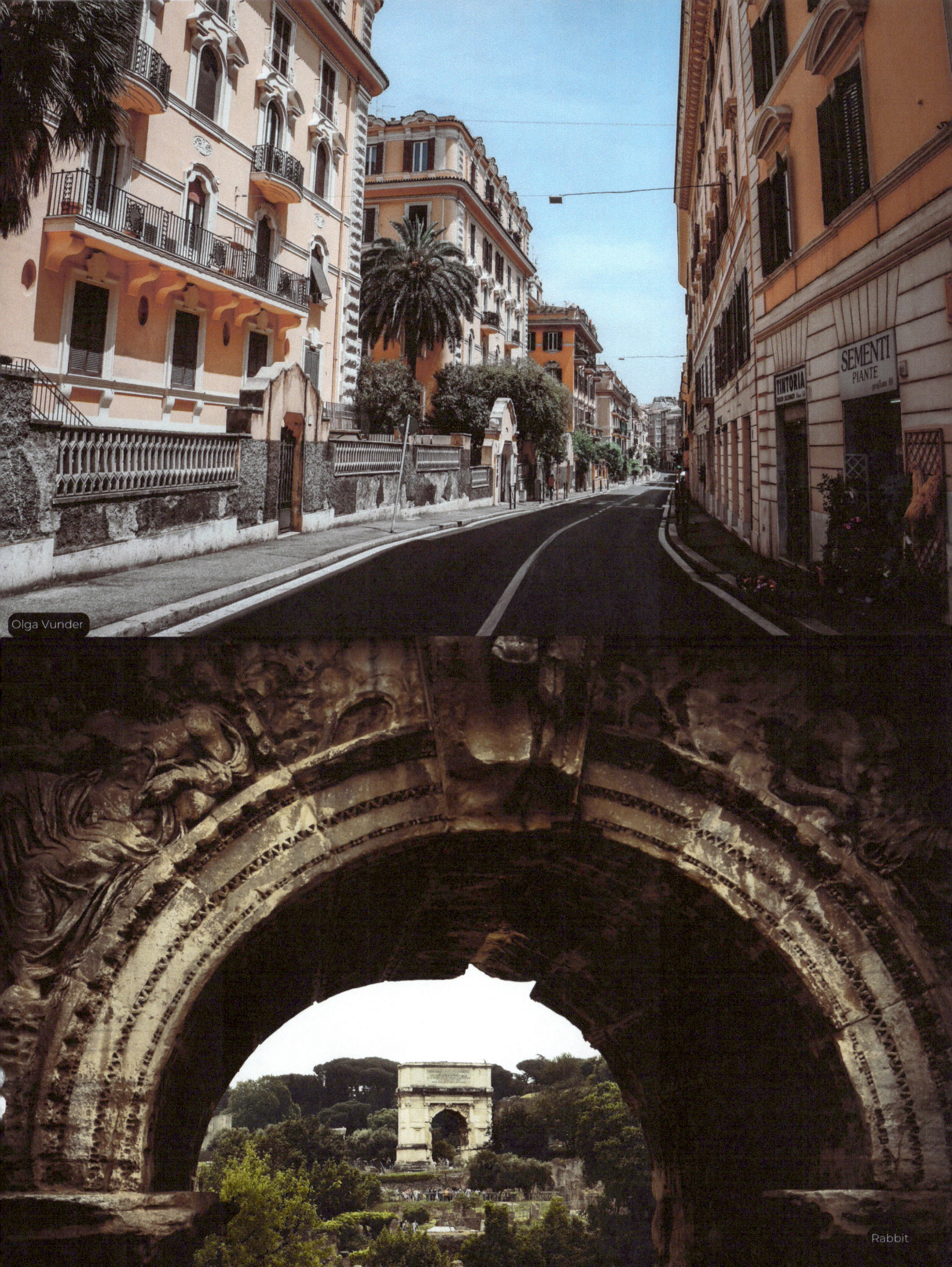

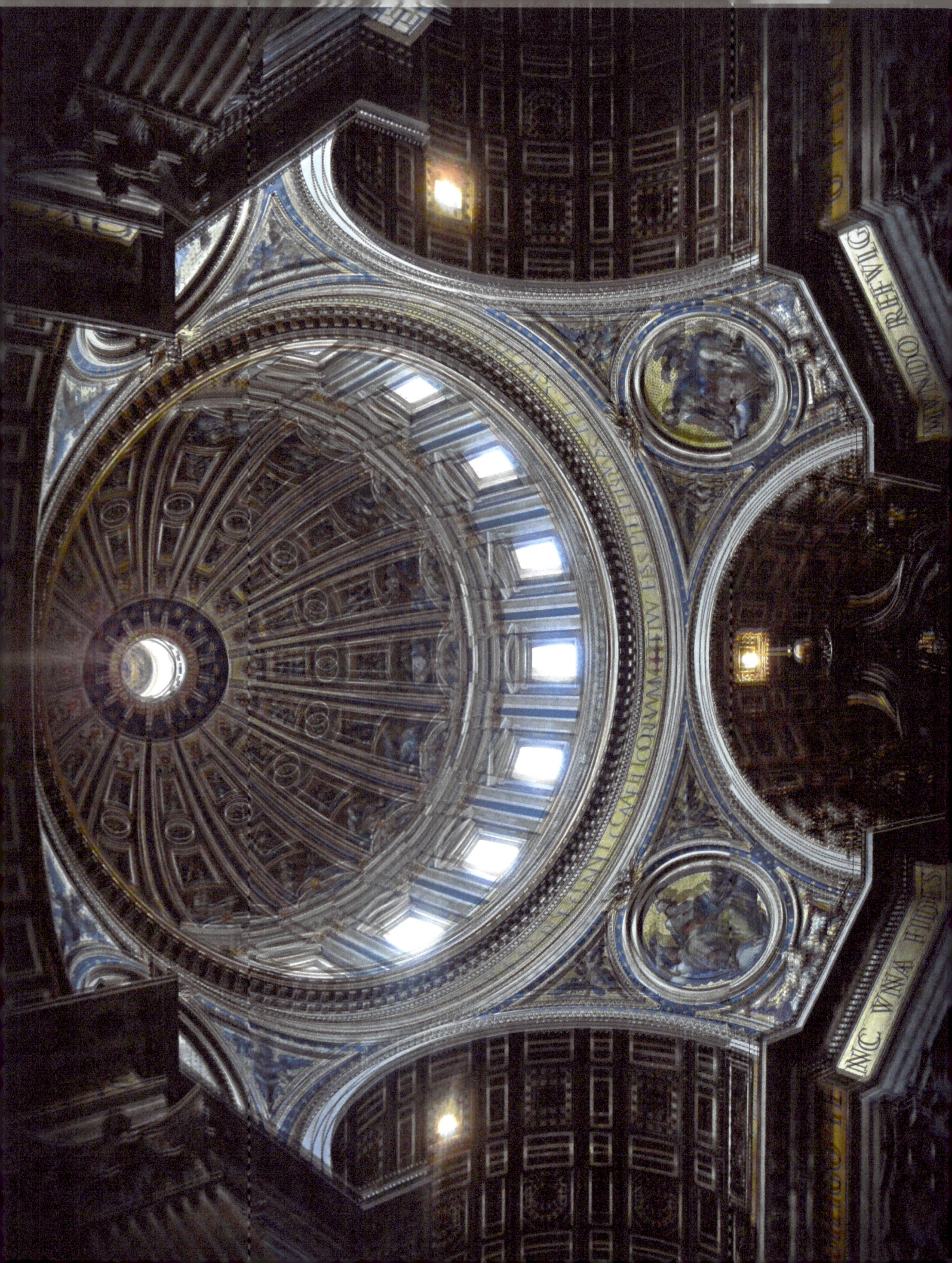

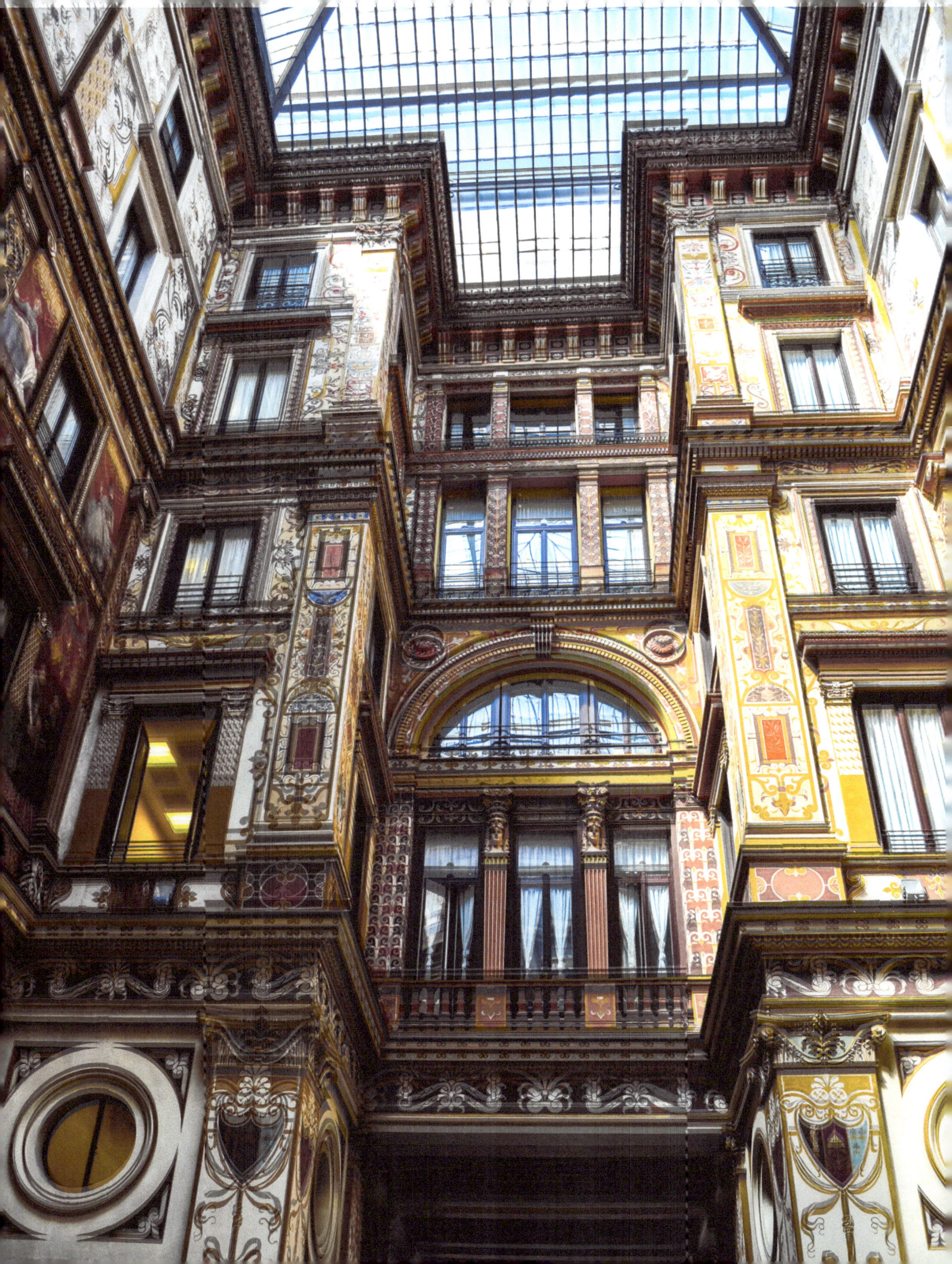

Colosseum

In the heart of Rome stands the Colosseum, an enduring symbol of the city's ancient prowess and architectural ingenuity. This colossal amphitheater, constructed in the 1st century AD under Emperor Vespasian, epitomizes the might of the Roman Empire. Its elliptical structure, spanning 189 meters in length and 156 meters in width, once hosted gladiatorial contests, public spectacles, and theatrical performances, captivating audiences of up to 50,000.

The Colosseum's exterior, a harmonious blend of travertine, tuff, and brick-faced concrete, showcases the Romans' mastery in engineering. Its four-story facade is adorned with a series of arches, framed by half-columns in the Doric, Ionic, and Corinthian orders, symbolizing the architectural evolution of the era.

Despite centuries of earthquakes and stone-robbery, the essence of its grandeur remains intact, whispering tales of a bygone era.

Inside, the arena's hypogeum, a complex network of tunnels and cages, once housed gladiators and animals before their dramatic entrance to the stage above. Today, the Colosseum stands partially ruined, yet its skeleton serves as a poignant reminder of Rome's historical narrative, a city where ancient and modern seamlessly intertwine. Exploring this monumental relic offers a glimpse into the soul of the Eternal City, a journey through time and history, where the echoes of ancient Rome still resonate.

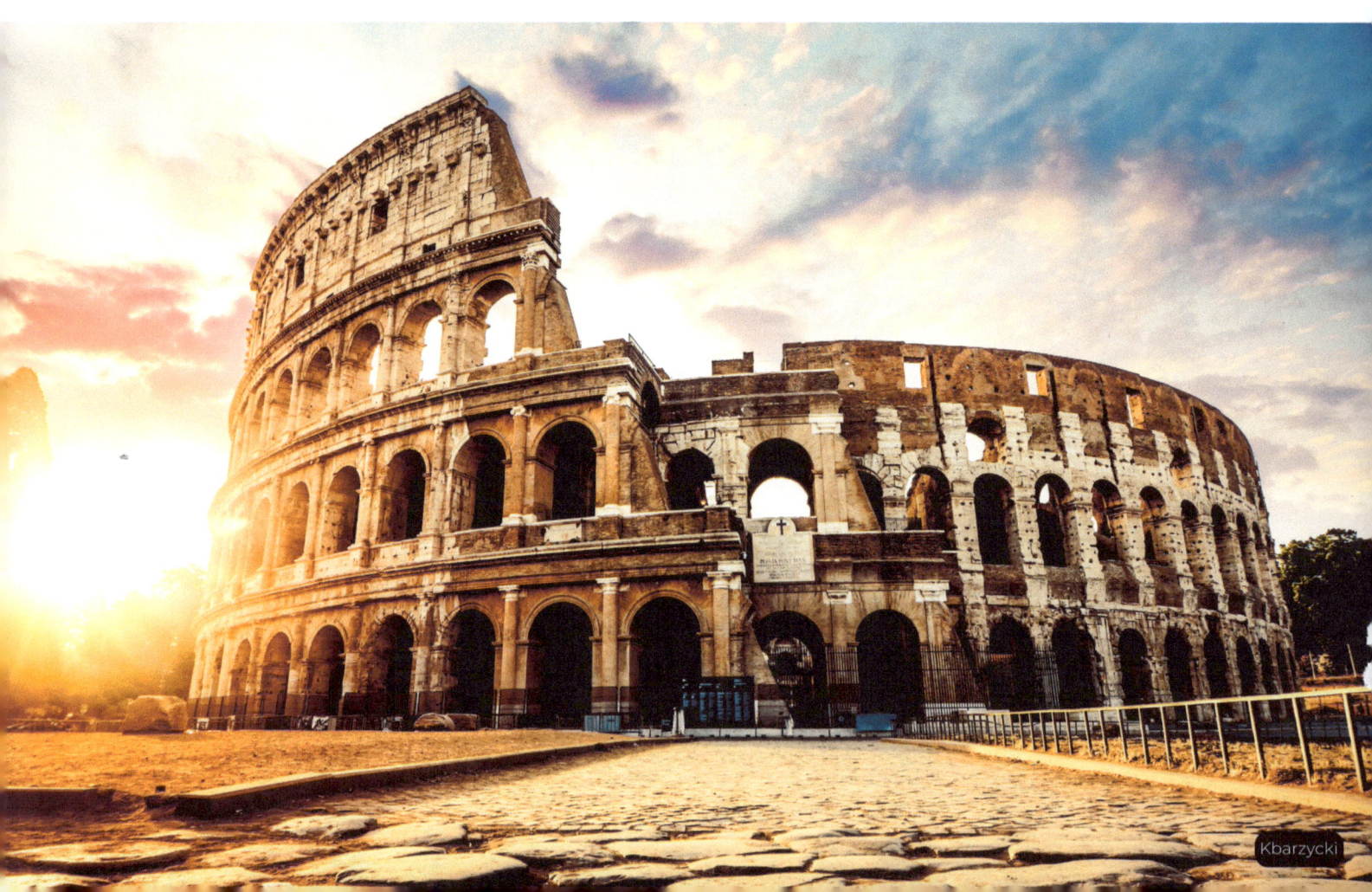

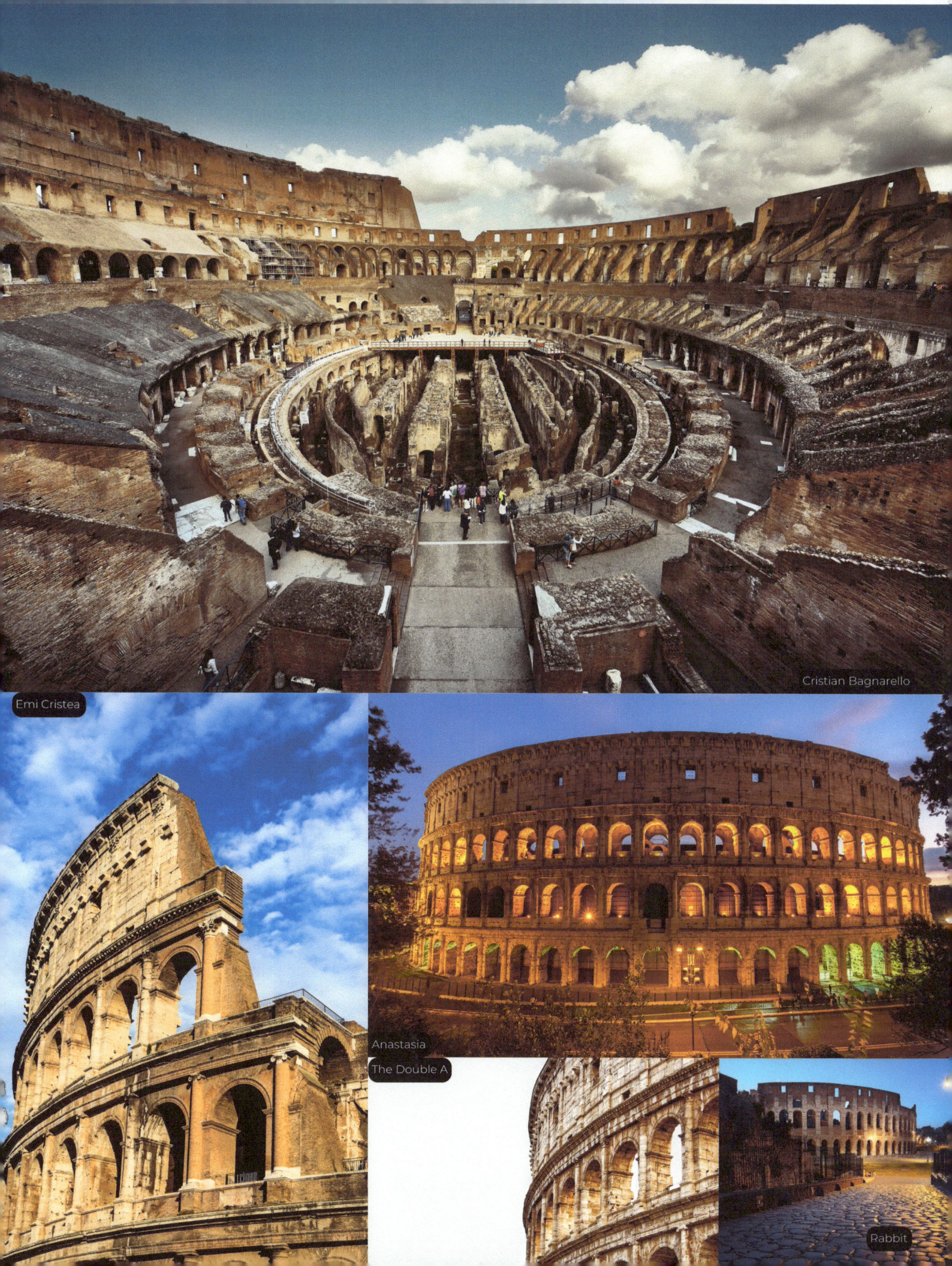

St. Peter's Basilica

St. Peter's Basilica, a pinnacle of Renaissance architecture, stands majestically in Vatican City, embodying the grandeur of Rome's spiritual heart. Conceived by legendary artists like Bramante, Michelangelo, and Bernini, its imposing façade, crowned by Michelangelo's iconic dome, heralds a sanctuary of profound artistry and religious significance. The basilica's interior, a cavernous expanse bathed in ethereal light, reveals a symphony of opulent marble, intricate stucco, and resplendent gold accents. The awe-inspiring Baldacchino, Bernini's masterpiece, rises with theatrical grace over the papal altar, encapsulating the fusion of art and faith.

As pilgrims and art aficionados meander through the nave, they encounter Michelangelo's poignant Pietà, a sculpture that captures the essence of Renaissance artistry and human emotion. The basilica's immense dome, a marvel of engineering, offers a heavenly perspective, its interior adorned with intricate frescoes leading the eye upwards in a metaphorical ascent to the divine. St. Peter's Basilica is not just a monument but a journey through centuries of religious devotion, artistic innovation, and cultural heritage, standing as a testament to Rome's enduring legacy as the Eternal City.

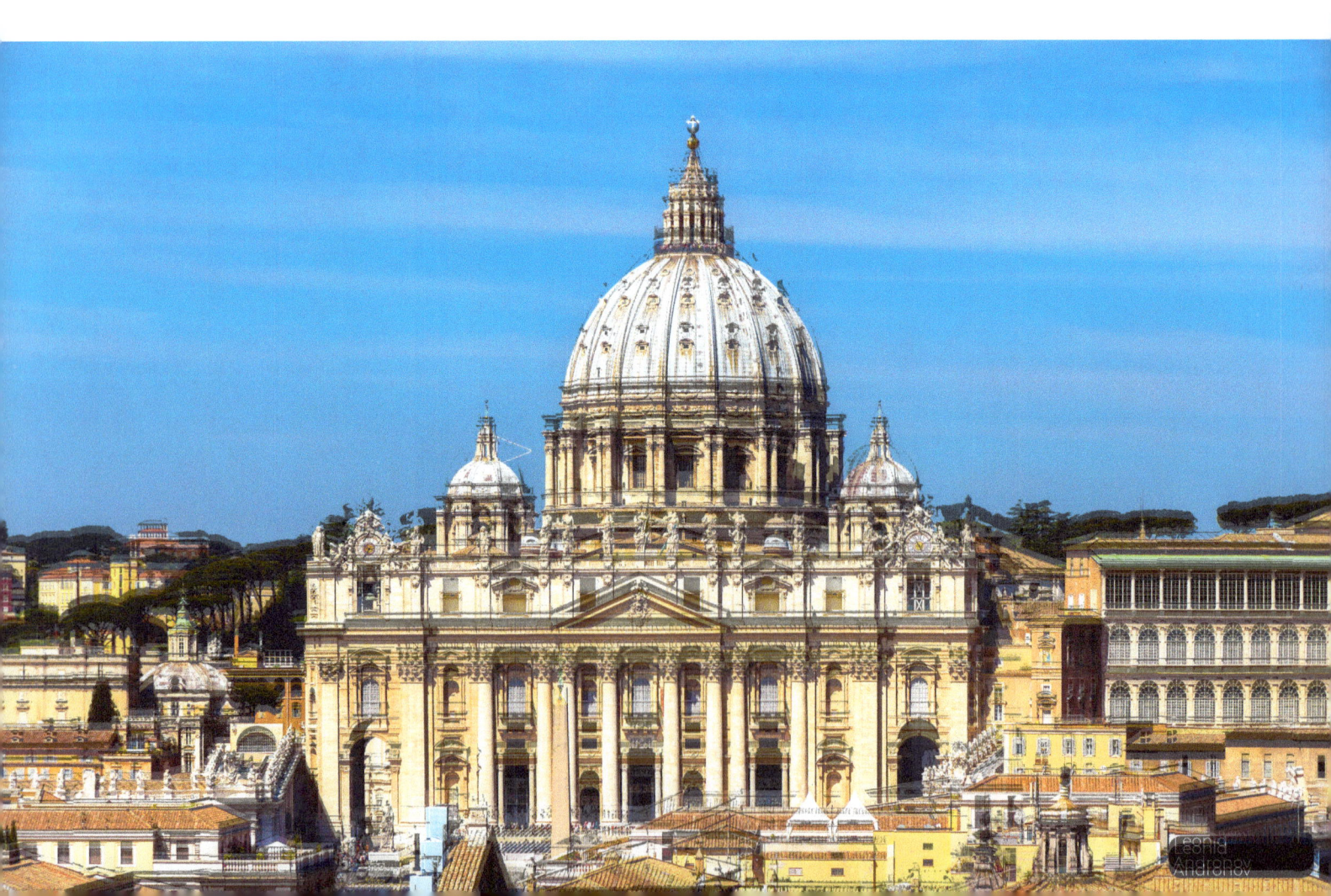

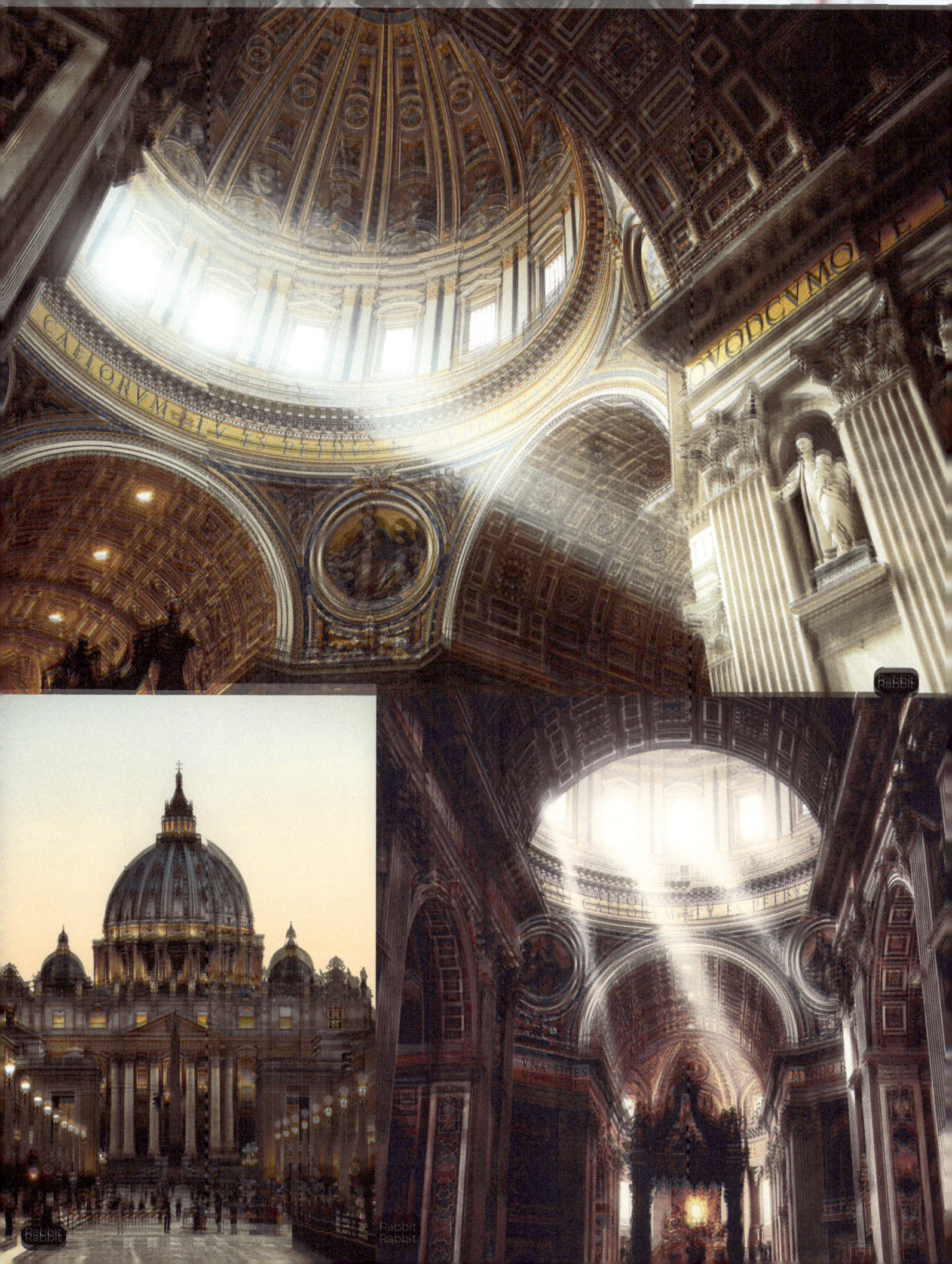

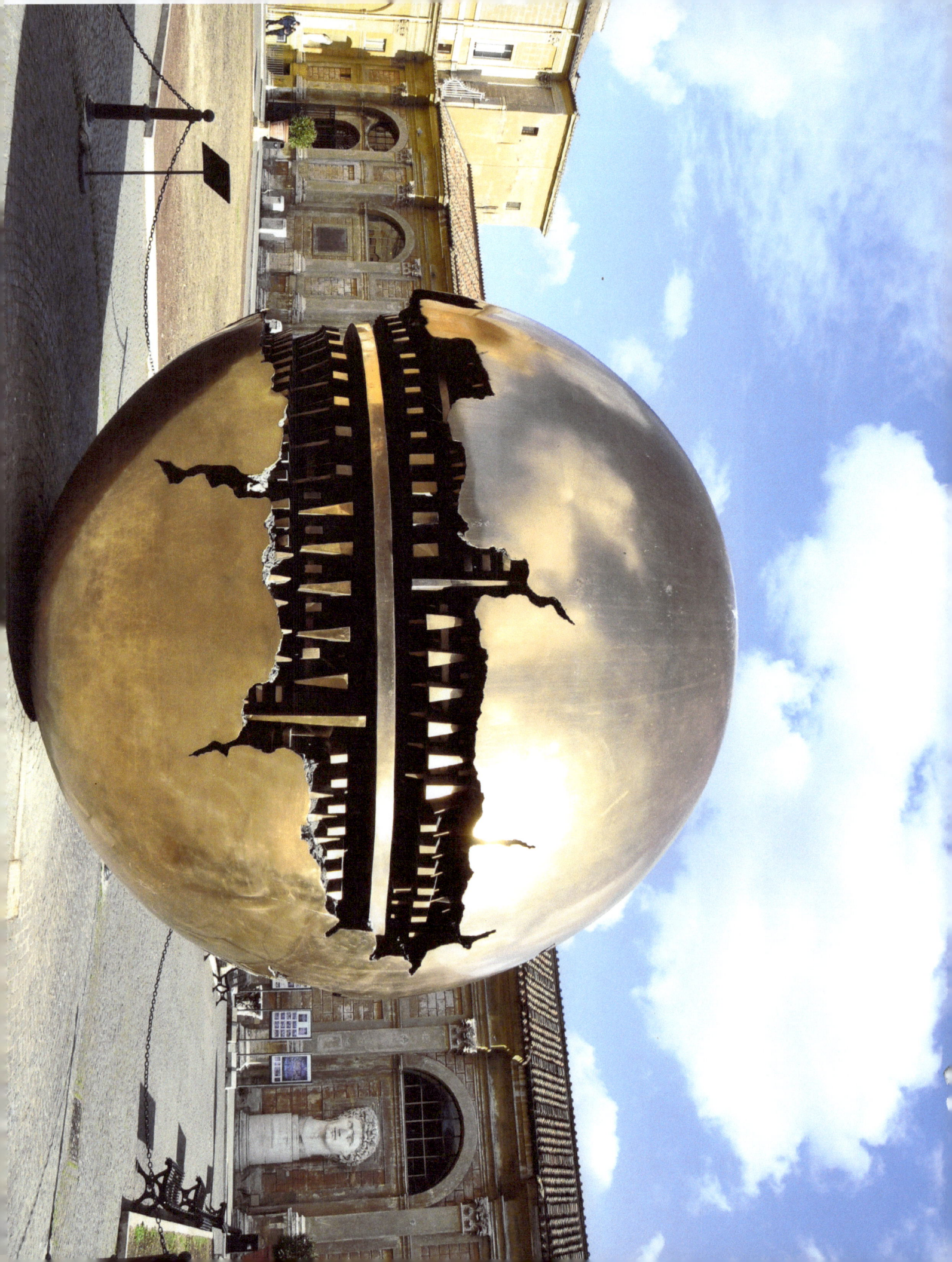

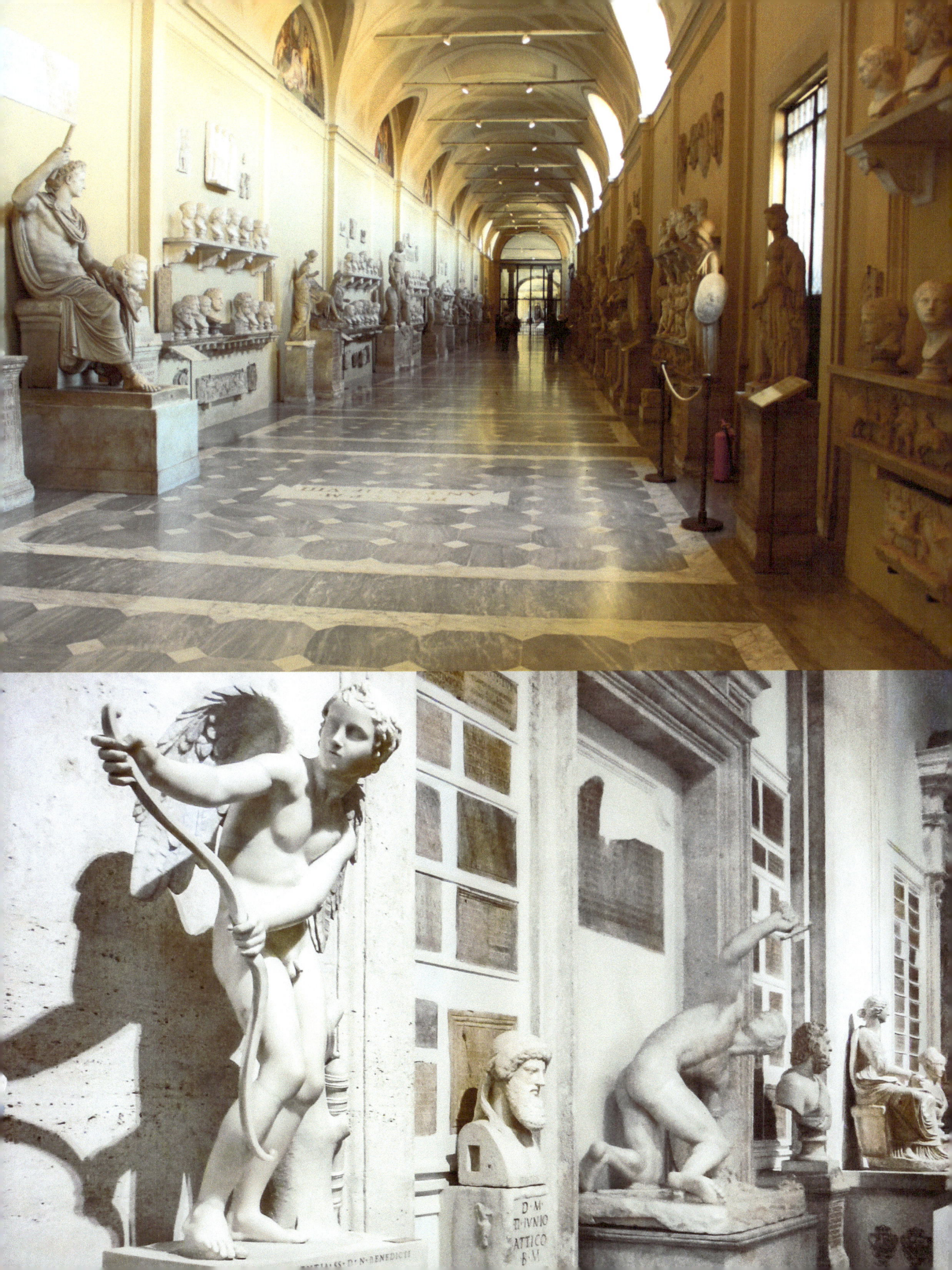

Trevi Fountain

The Trevi Fountain, an architectural jewel in Rome's historic heart, is a baroque masterpiece of art and myth. Designed by Nicola Salvi in the 18th century and completed by Giuseppe Pannini, it's not just a fountain but a grand theatrical stage set against the Palazzo Poli. At its core, the majestic figure of Oceanus, god of all waters, emerges triumphantly, flanked by tritons and sea horses that embody the shifting moods of the sea.

The fountain's elaborate sculptures weave a narrative of Neptune's dominion, framed by faux rocks and cascading waters that create a dynamic interplay of sound and light. This immersive tableau captivates onlookers, drawing them into a world where art and legend intertwine. The fountain's allure extends beyond its visual grandeur, encapsulated in the tradition of tossing a coin over one's shoulder, promising a return to Rome, a city etched in history and romance.

By night, the Trevi Fountain transforms, its illuminated waters casting ethereal reflections, creating an ambiance of enchantment. This iconic site, more than a monument, is a celebration of artistic genius, a testament to Rome's enduring splendor, and a gathering place where stories, dreams, and the timeless charm of the Eternal City converge in a spectacular dance of water and stone.

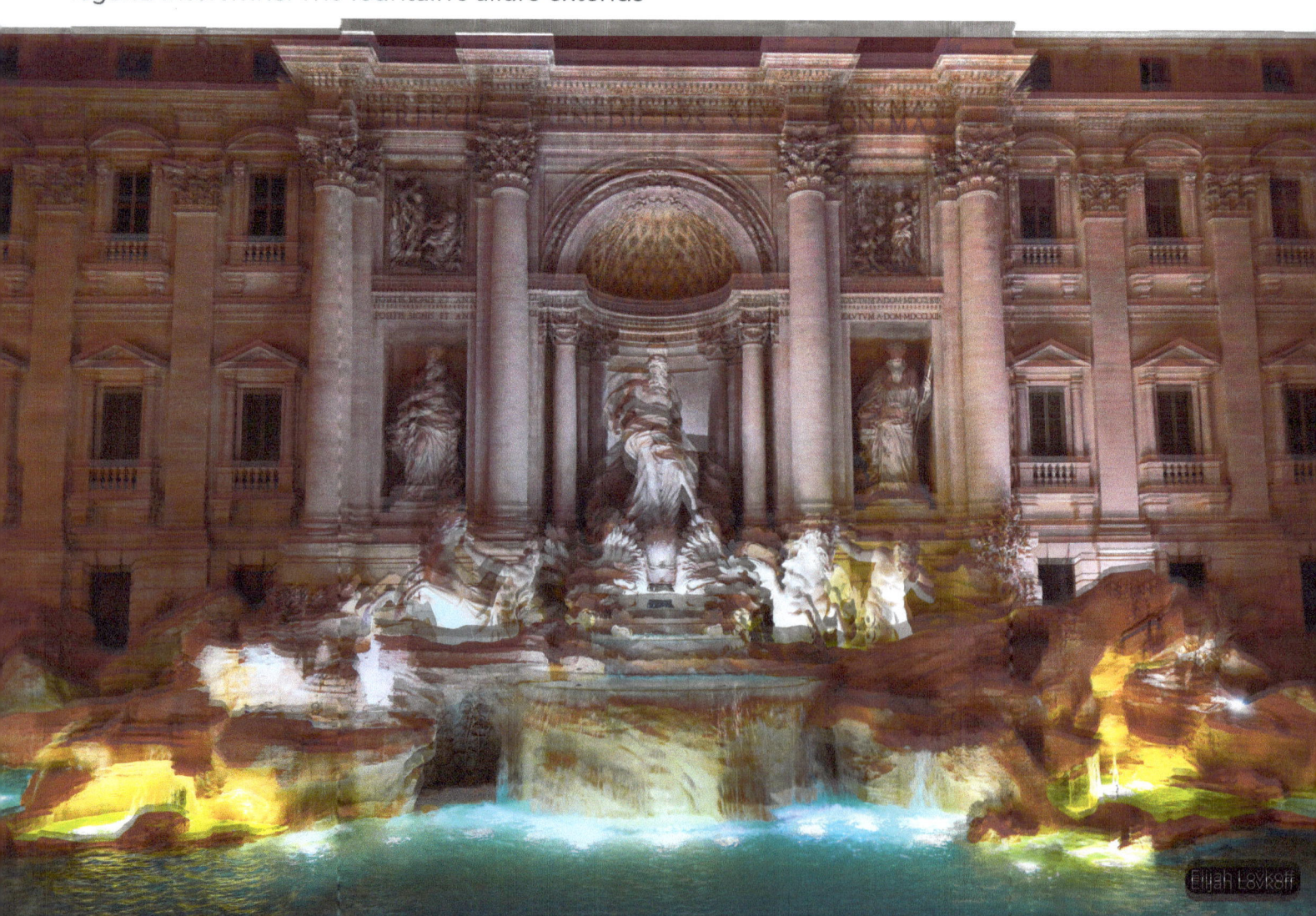

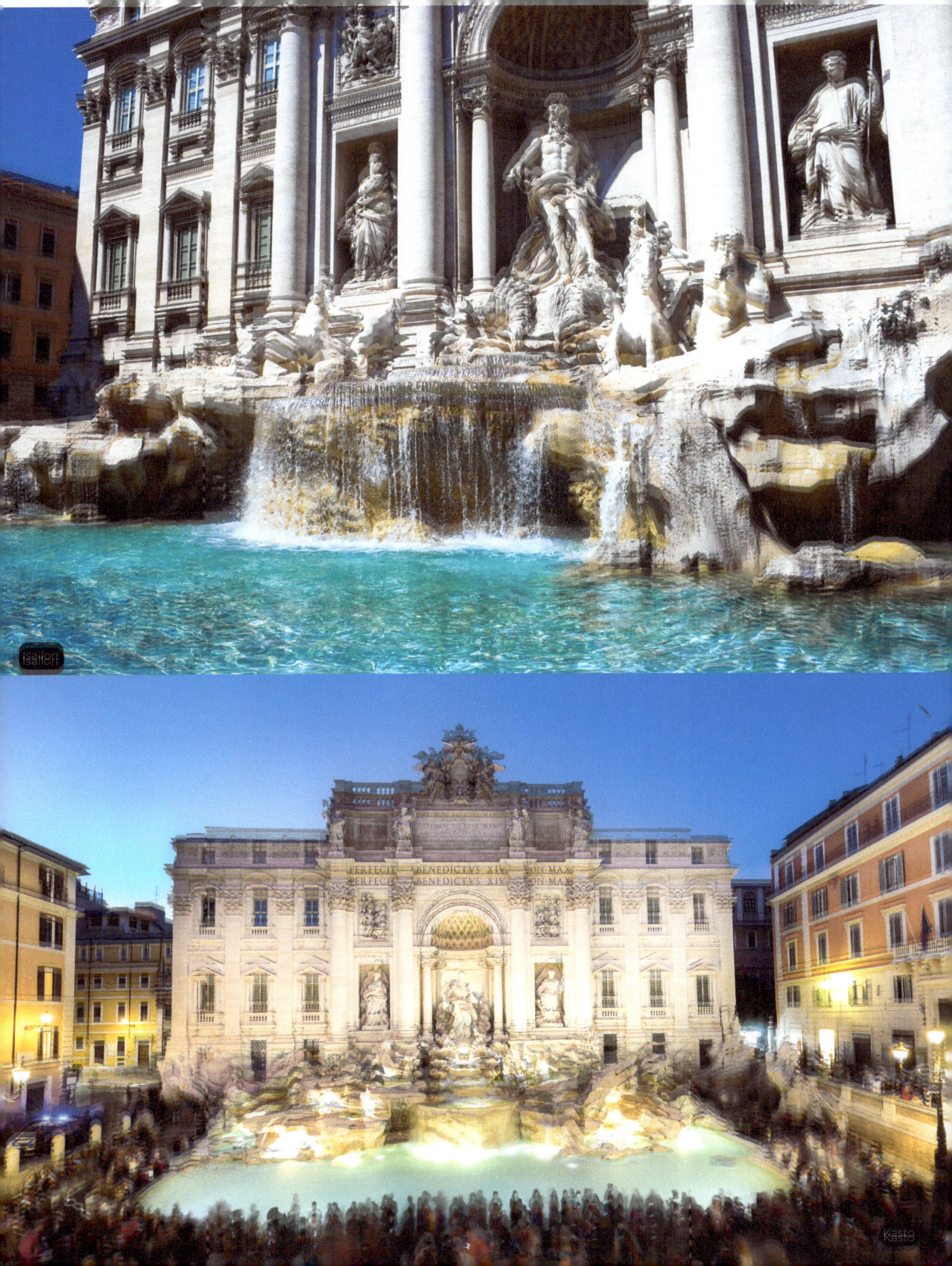

Castel Sant'Angelo

Castel Sant'Angelo, originally the Mausoleum of Hadrian, stands as a fortress of history and legend on the banks of the Tiber River in Rome. This cylindrical building, constructed in 135 AD, has evolved through the ages, serving as a mausoleum, a fortress, a papal residence, and now a museum. Its architectural layers narrate Rome's tumultuous history, from the splendor of the Roman Empire to the intrigues of the Renaissance papacy.

The castle's robust exterior, crowned with the statue of Archangel Michael – a symbol of the end of the plague in Rome – holds within it a complex labyrinth of rooms and corridors. Each chamber unfolds stories of the past, from lavish Renaissance frescoes to somber prison cells.

The Passetto di Borgo, a secret passageway connecting the castle to the Vatican, whispers tales of papal escapades and narrow escapes.

From the top, visitors are greeted with a panoramic vista of Rome, a breathtaking sweep from the winding Tiber to the dome of St. Peter's Basilica. Castel Sant'Angelo, with its rich tapestry of history, art, and legend, is not just a monument but a journey through time, offering a unique glimpse into the layers of Rome's ceaselessly evolving narrative.

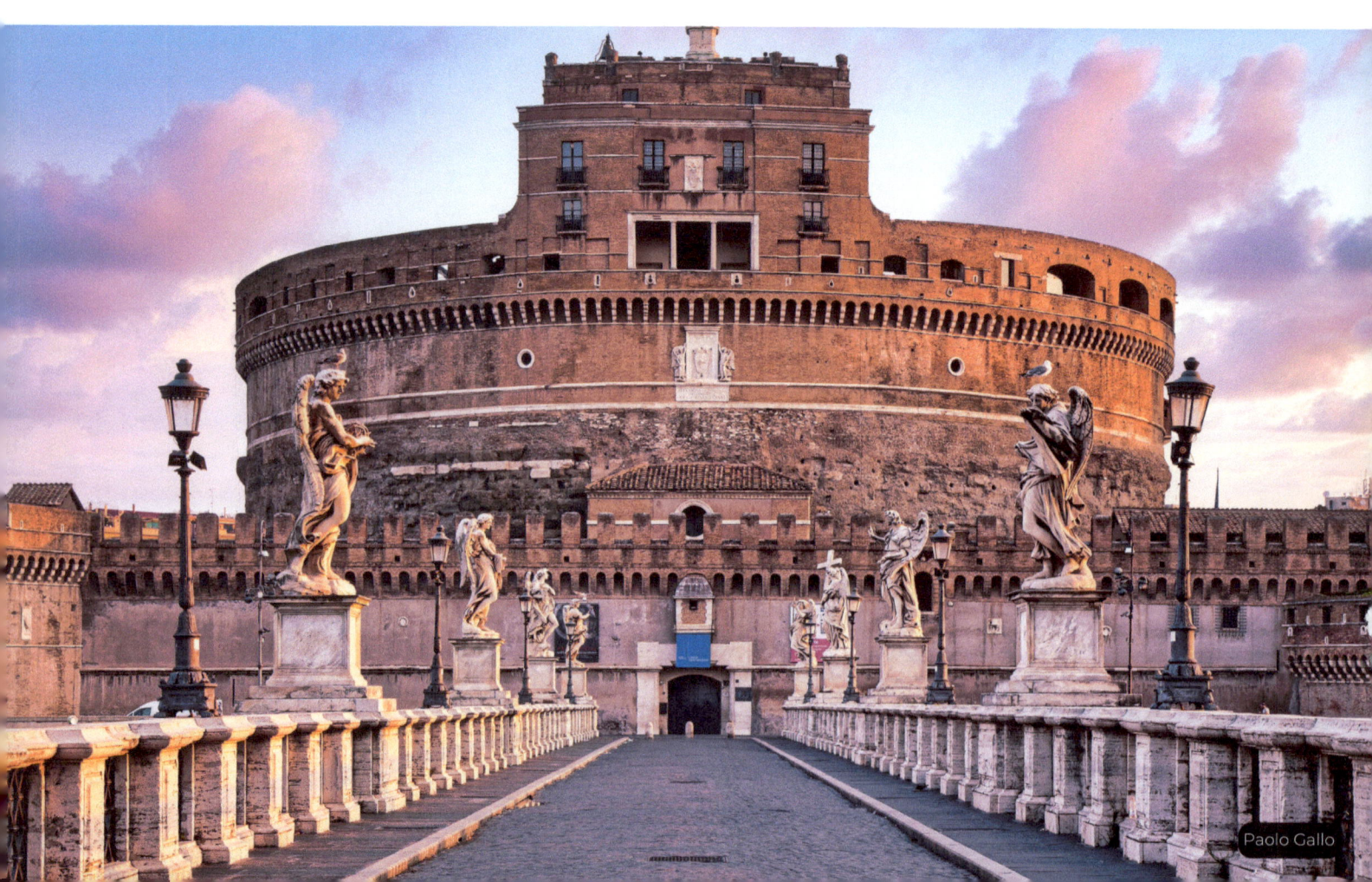

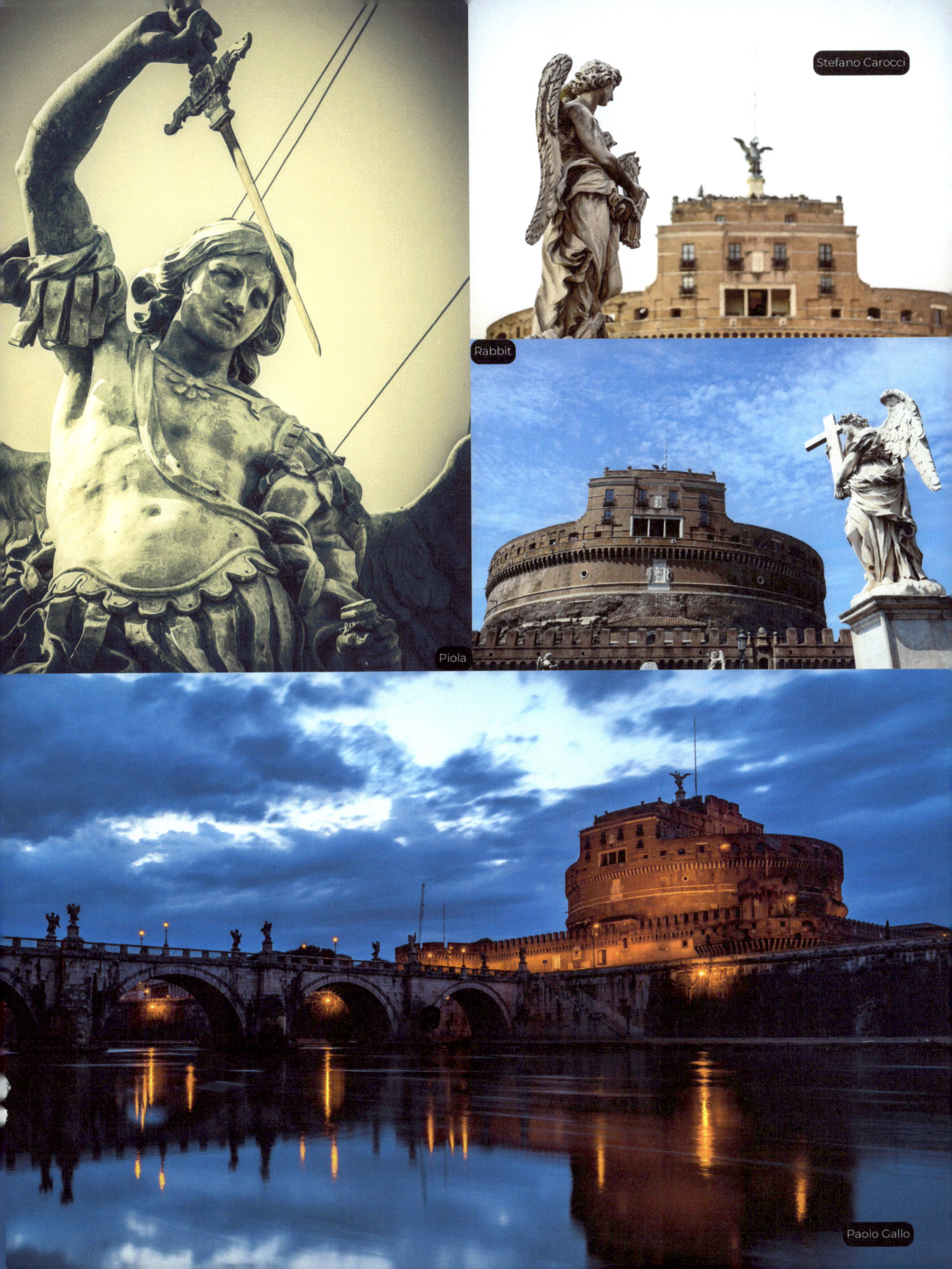

Pantheon

The Pantheon, a marvel of ancient Roman architecture, stands resiliently in the bustling heart of Rome. Originally built by Marcus Agrippa and later rebuilt by Emperor Hadrian around 126 AD, this architectural masterpiece has withstood the ravages of time, symbolizing the grandeur of the Roman Empire. The Pantheon's imposing façade, marked by grand Corinthian columns, ushers visitors into a realm of historical wonder.

Its most striking feature, the massive dome, a feat of engineering genius, holds the title of the world's largest unreinforced concrete dome. The oculus at the dome's apex, a unique architectural element, opens to the sky, creating a harmonious interplay of light and space within. This celestial opening not only illuminates the Pantheon's interior but also symbolizes the temple's dedication to all gods of ancient Rome.

The interior, a testament to the extraordinary craftsmanship of Roman builders, showcases a perfect harmony of proportions. The Pantheon's enduring beauty extends to its role as a final resting place for eminent figures like Raphael and Italian kings.

Standing in the Pantheon, enveloped by its ancient, sacred aura, visitors are transported across centuries, bearing witness to an enduring legacy that intertwines Roman history, architectural innovation, and timeless beauty.

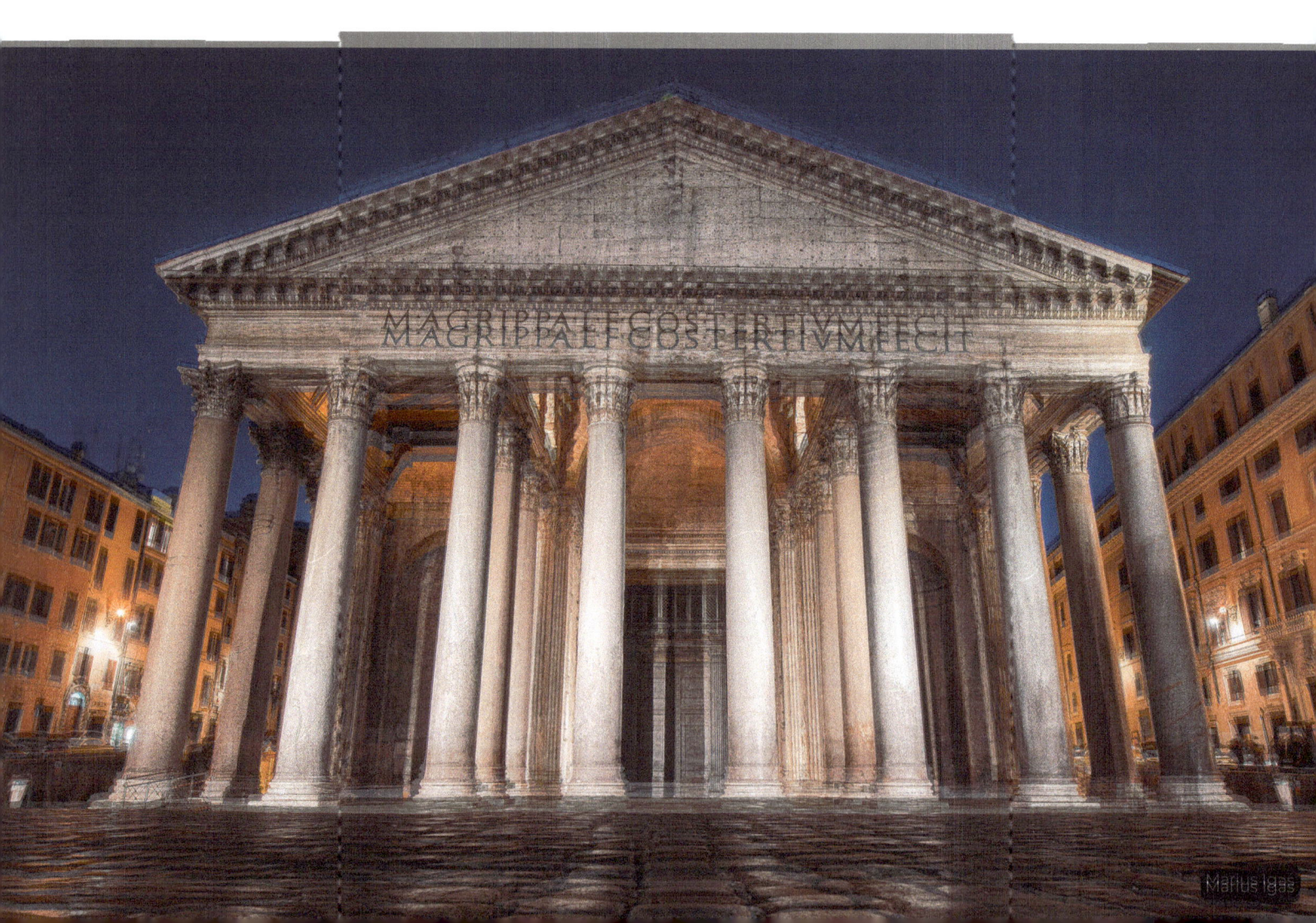

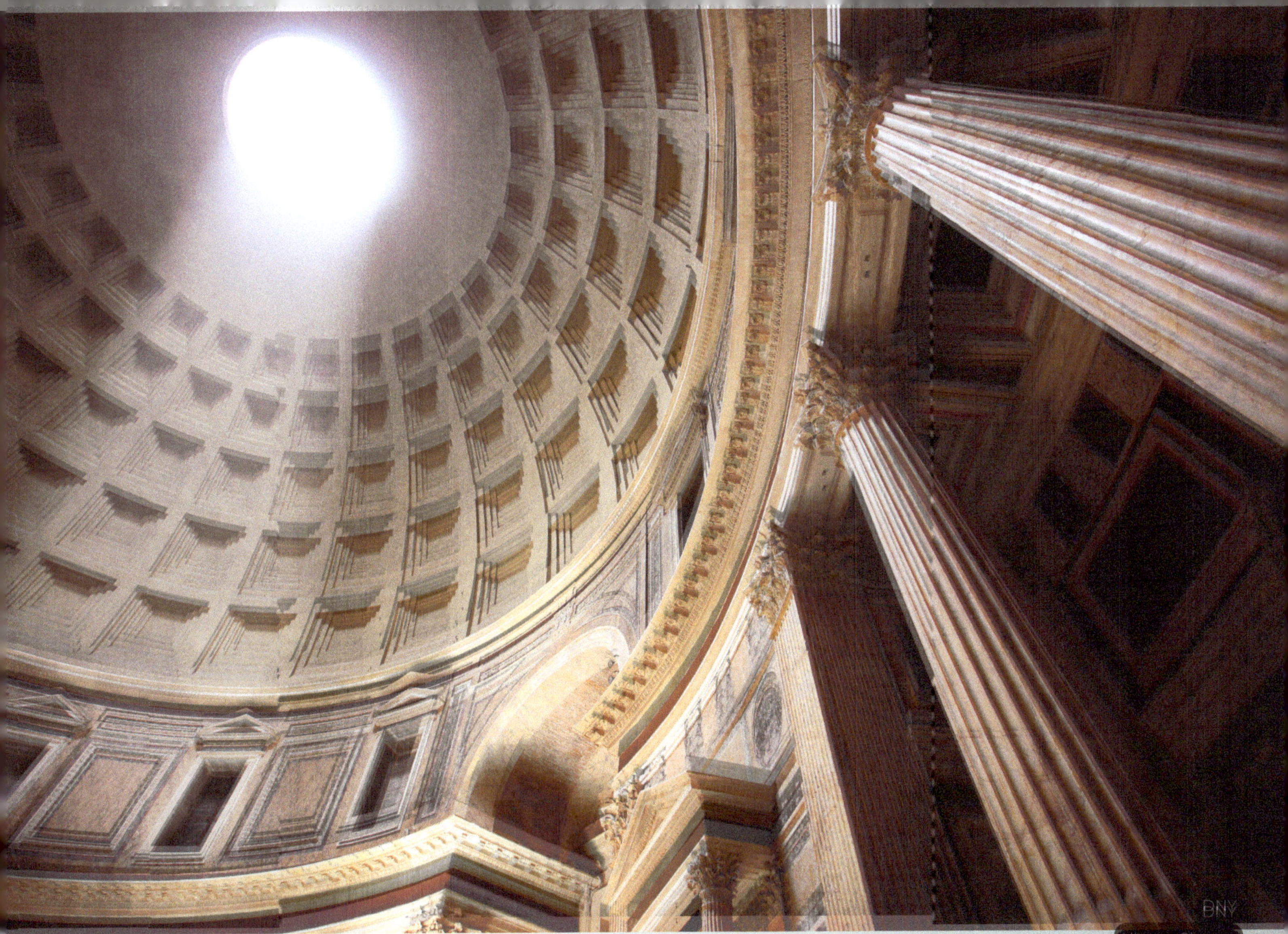

M·AGRIPPA·L·F·COS·TERTIVM·FECIT

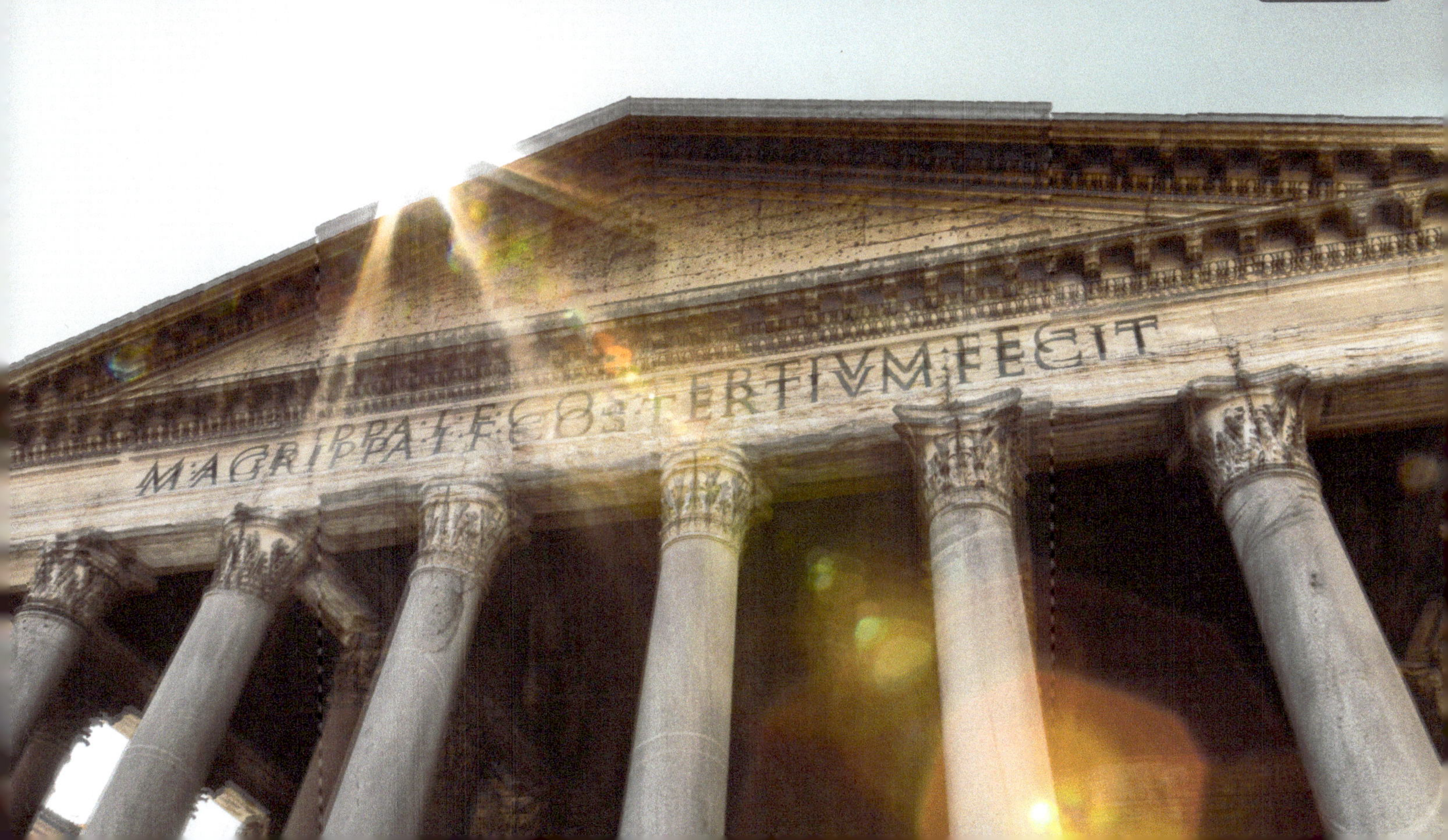

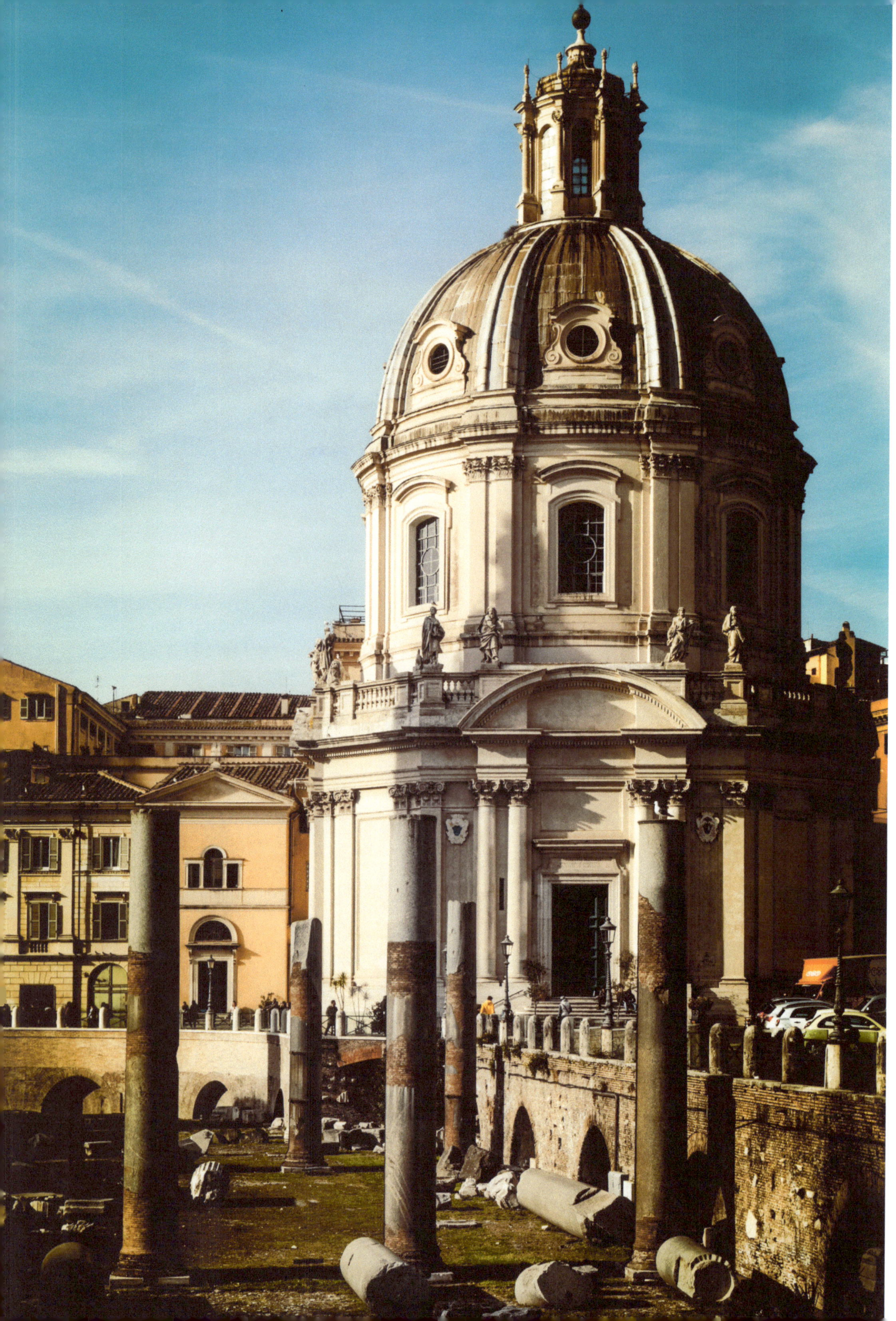

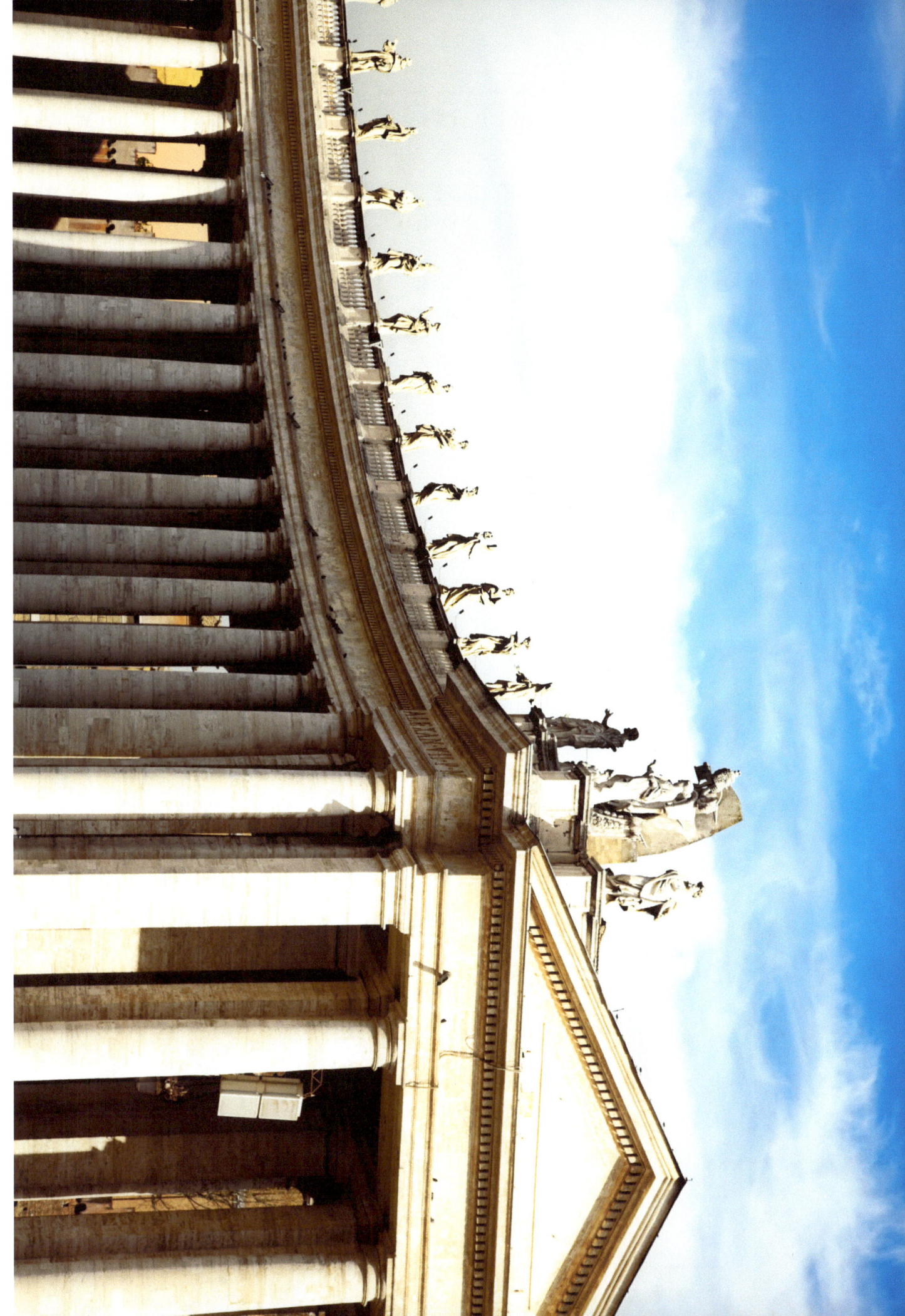

Roman Forum

The Roman Forum, a sprawling tapestry of ruins in the heart of Rome, is a testament to the grandeur of the Roman Empire. Once the epicenter of Roman public life, it held temples, markets, and the seat of government. Today, it offers a window into ancient history, where each stone whispers tales of glory and decline.

Walking through the Forum is like traversing time. The Temple of Saturn, with its remaining iconic columns, evokes the splendor of early Roman religion. The Curia, the ancient Senate House, still stands, echoing with the imagined debates of senators. The Via Sacra, the main thoroughfare, is where triumphant generals once paraded with their legions.

Amid these ruins, the Arch of Titus stands majestically, commemorating the Roman victory in Jerusalem. The Forum's scattered fragments — columns, arches, and stones — are puzzle pieces of history, painting a vivid picture of Roman life, politics, and culture.

The Roman Forum is not merely a collection of ruins but a sanctuary of memory and history, a place where the past feels tangible. It invites visitors to ponder the rise and fall of empires, offering a poignant reflection on power, time, and the enduring legacy of one of the world's greatest civilizations.

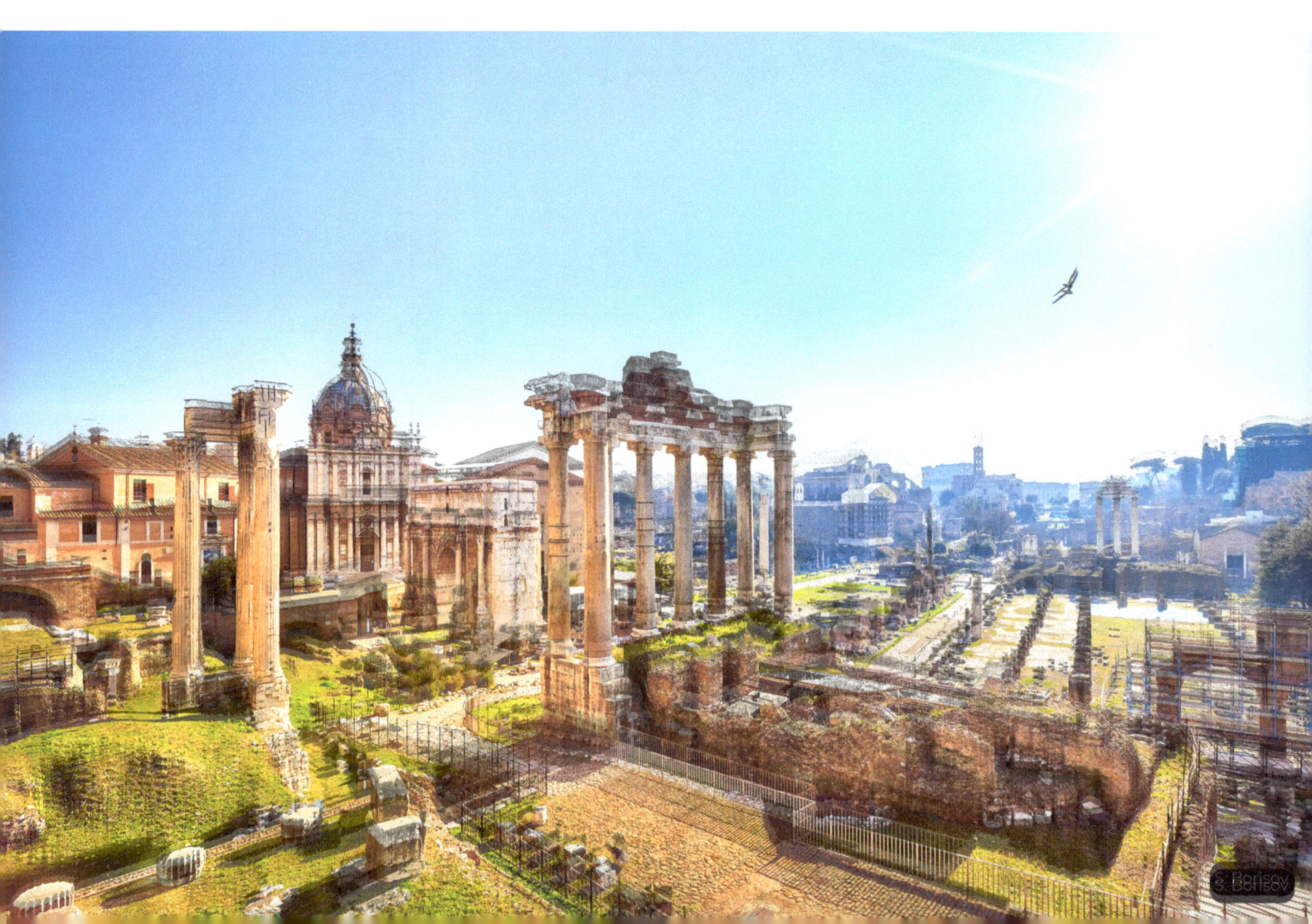

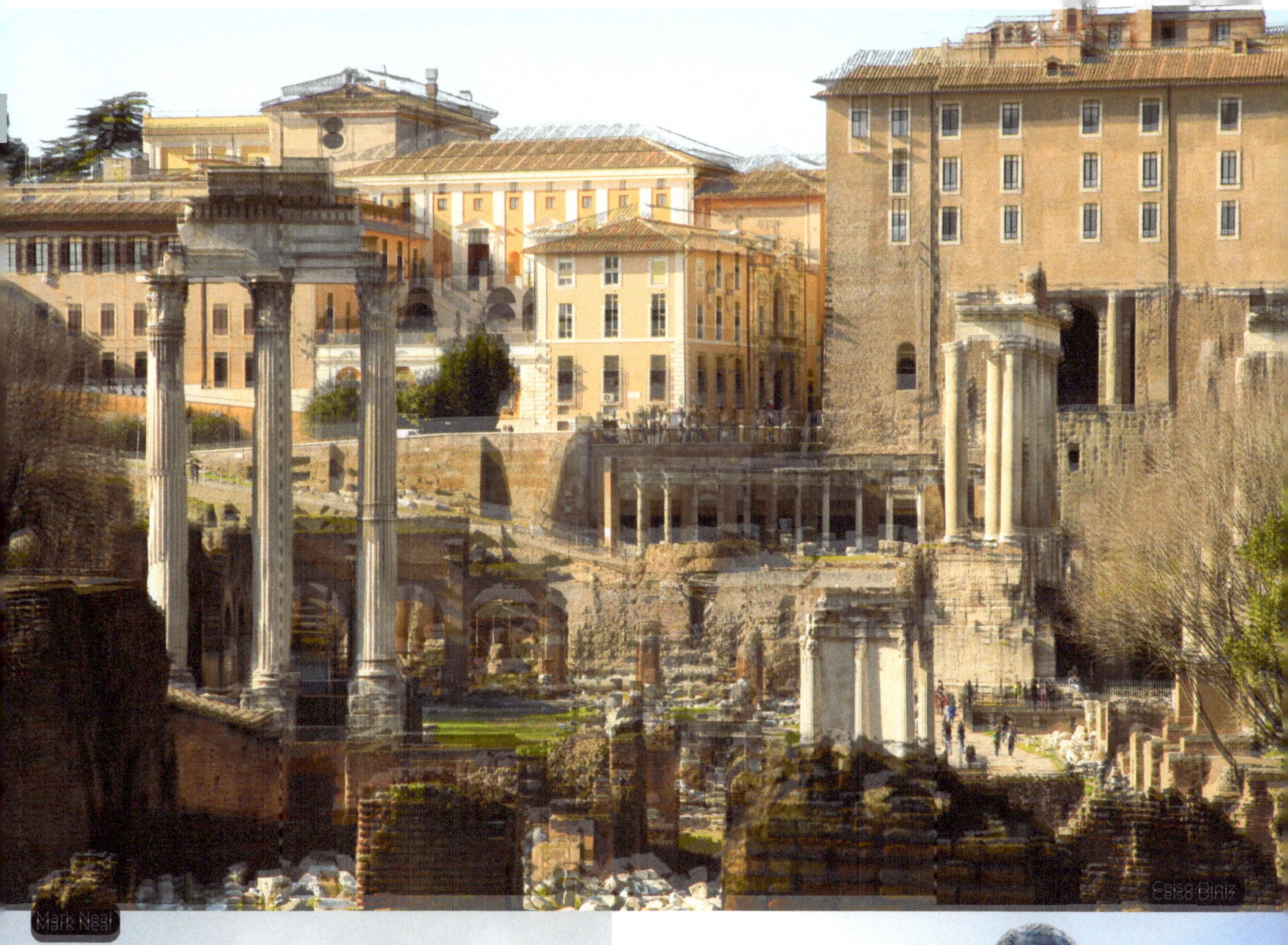

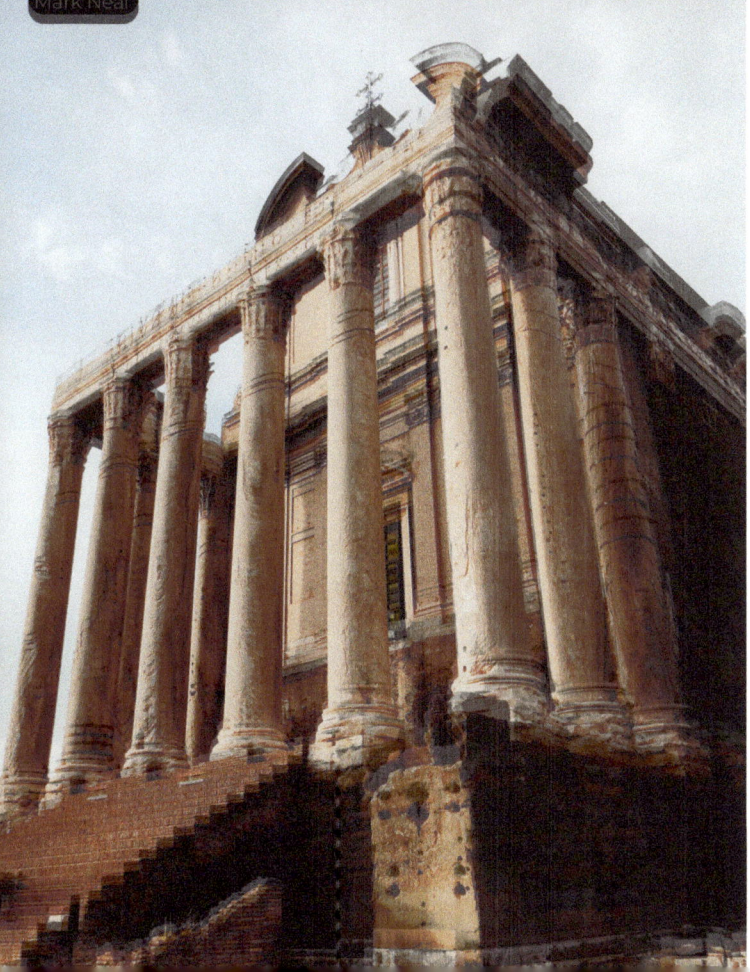
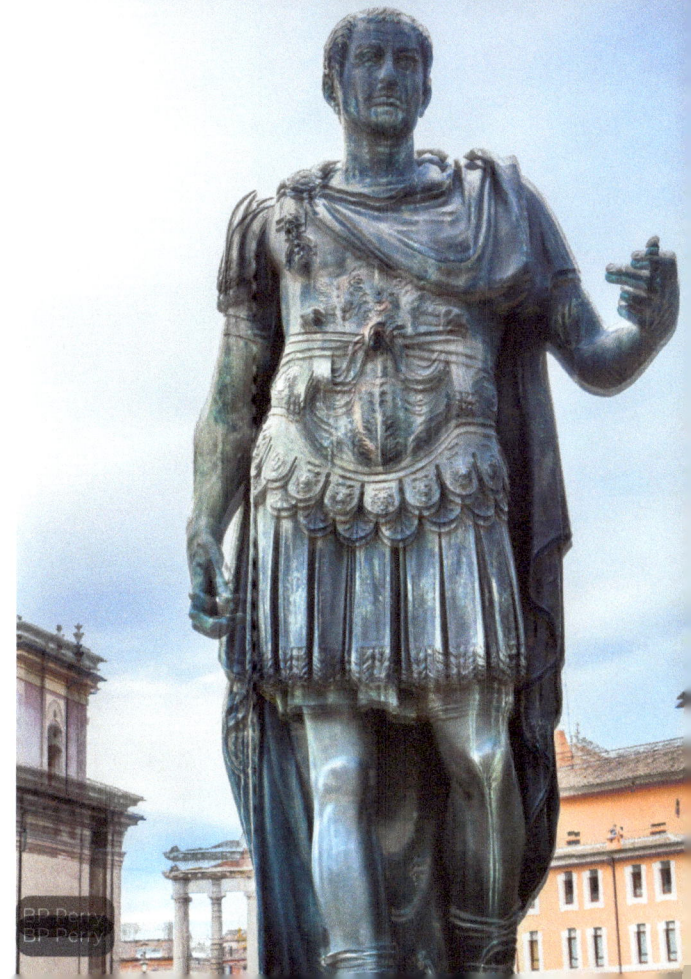

Gardens of the Vatican

The Vatican Gardens, an oasis of tranquility nestled within the heart of Vatican City, are a hidden gem of lush greenery and historical significance. Spanning approximately 23 hectares, these gardens represent a serene retreat from the bustling streets of Rome, offering a spiritual and visual journey through beautifully manicured landscapes and a rich tapestry of history.

Established during the Renaissance and Baroque periods, the gardens are a harmonious blend of nature and artistry. They feature a variety of flora, ranging from classical Italian gardens with neatly trimmed hedges to more informal arrangements, creating a mosaic of botanical beauty.

Interspersed among the greenery are fountains, sculptures, and grottoes, each adding a layer of elegance and history.

The Vatican Gardens also house several important religious sites, including the Lourdes Grotto, a replica of the famed French shrine, providing a space for contemplation and prayer. The meticulous layout of the gardens, with paths winding through the lush vegetation, invites visitors on a meditative journey through both the sacred and the natural world.

A visit to the Vatican Gardens is a foray into a lesser-known aspect of Vatican City, offering a unique perspective on the blend of spiritual, cultural, and natural beauty that defines this sovereign city-state within Rome.

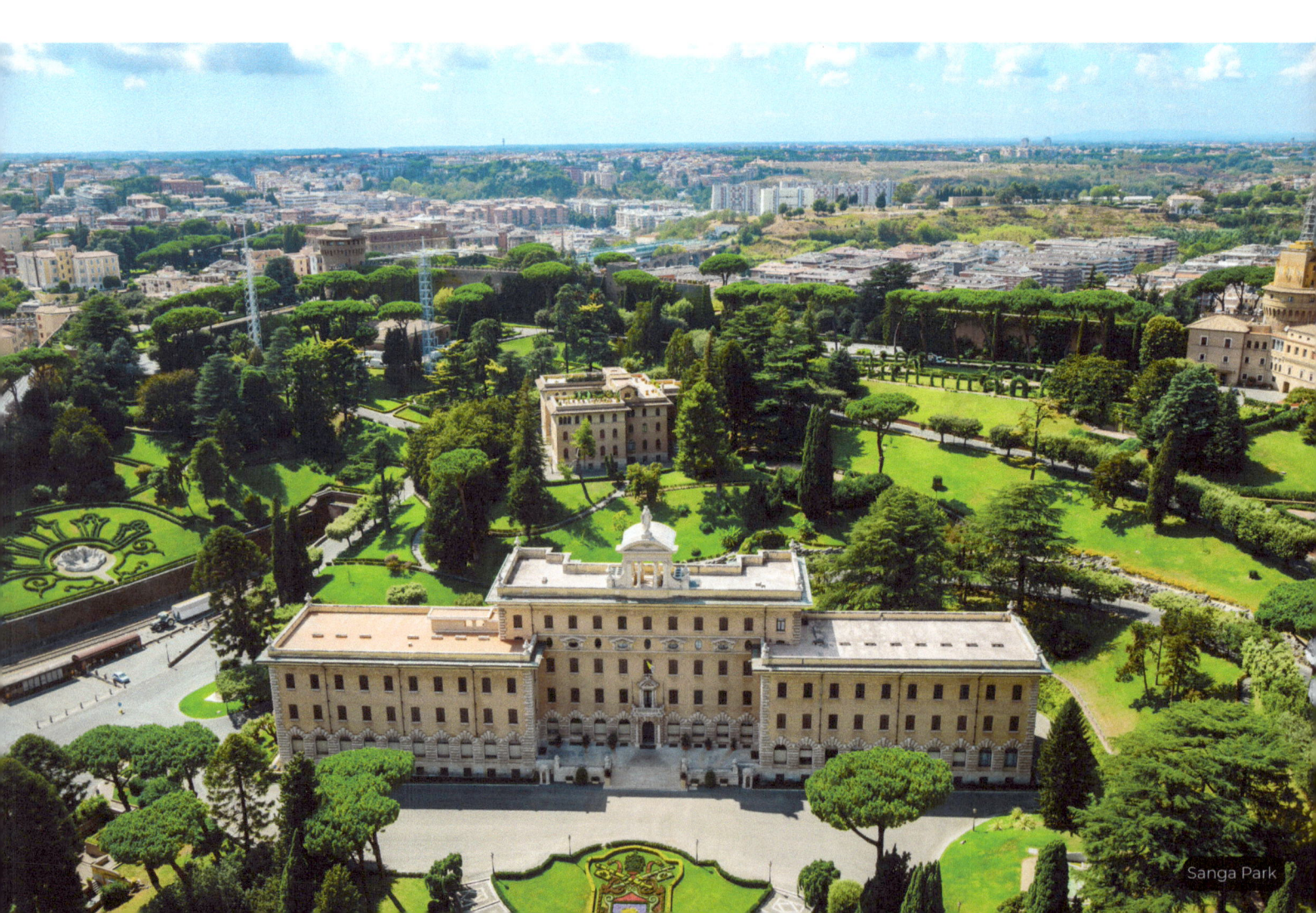

Sanga Park

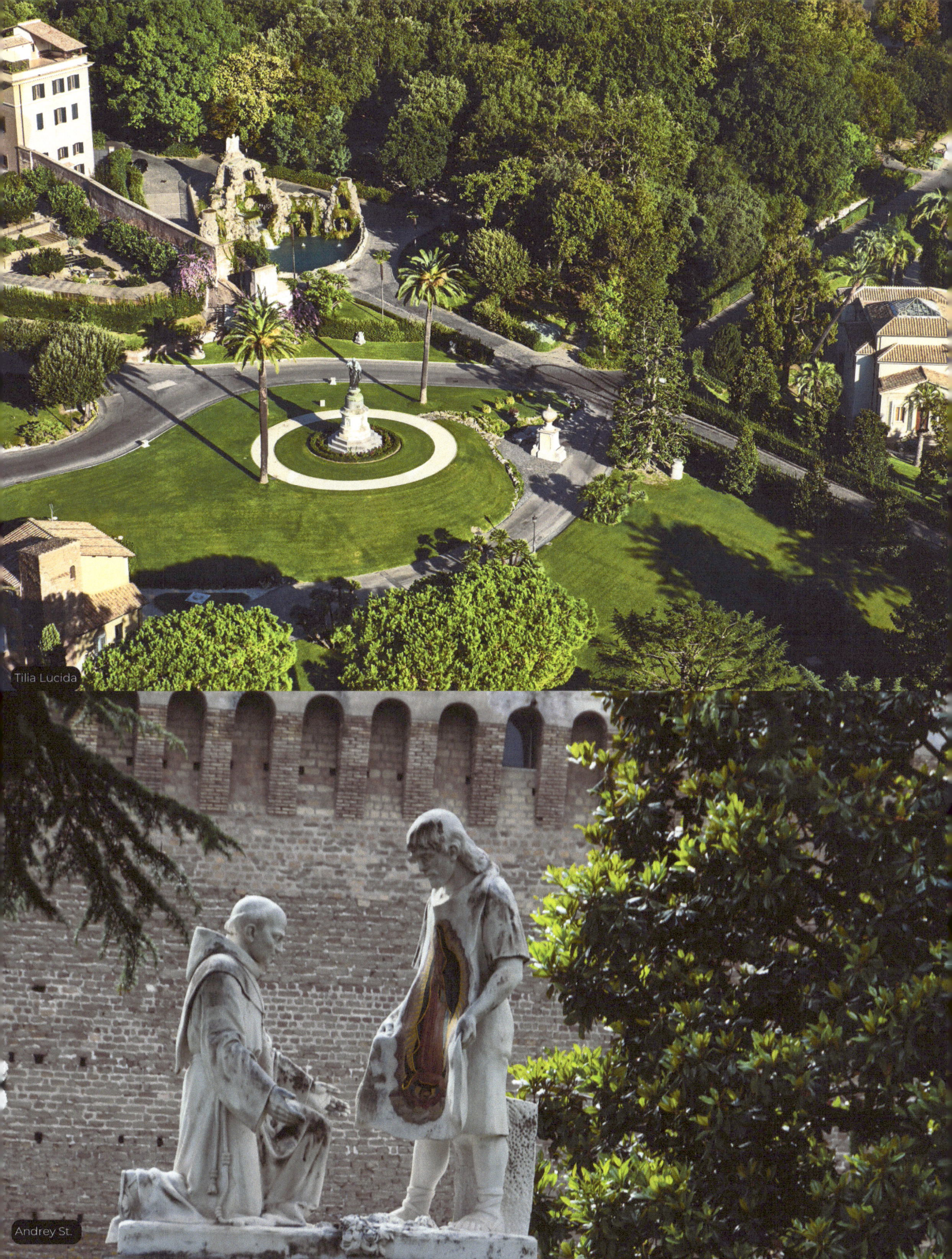

Vatican City

Vatican City, the world's smallest independent state, is an enclave of spiritual and artistic grandeur nestled in the heart of Rome. This sovereign city-state, the seat of the Roman Catholic Church and home to the Pope, is a place where history, faith, and art converge in a breathtaking display. Spanning just over 44 hectares, it packs an immense cultural and religious significance within its walls.

At the heart of Vatican City stands the majestic St. Peter's Basilica, an architectural marvel and a pilgrimage site for the faithful from around the globe. The basilica, with its iconic dome designed by Michelangelo, houses priceless works of art, including Michelangelo's Pietà and Bernini's Baldacchino. Adjacent to the basilica is the sprawling St. Peter's Square, a masterpiece of baroque design, where thousands gather to receive the Pope's blessings.

The Vatican Museums offer a journey through centuries of art, including the Raphael Rooms and the incomparable Sistine Chapel, renowned for Michelangelo's ceiling and The Last Judgment fresco. Beyond the spiritual and artistic allure, the Vatican's Apostolic Palace, manicured gardens, and ancient archives add layers to its mystique.

Vatican City is not just a destination; it's an experience of awe and inspiration, encapsulating the essence of art, religion, and history in an unparalleled microcosm of cultural richness.

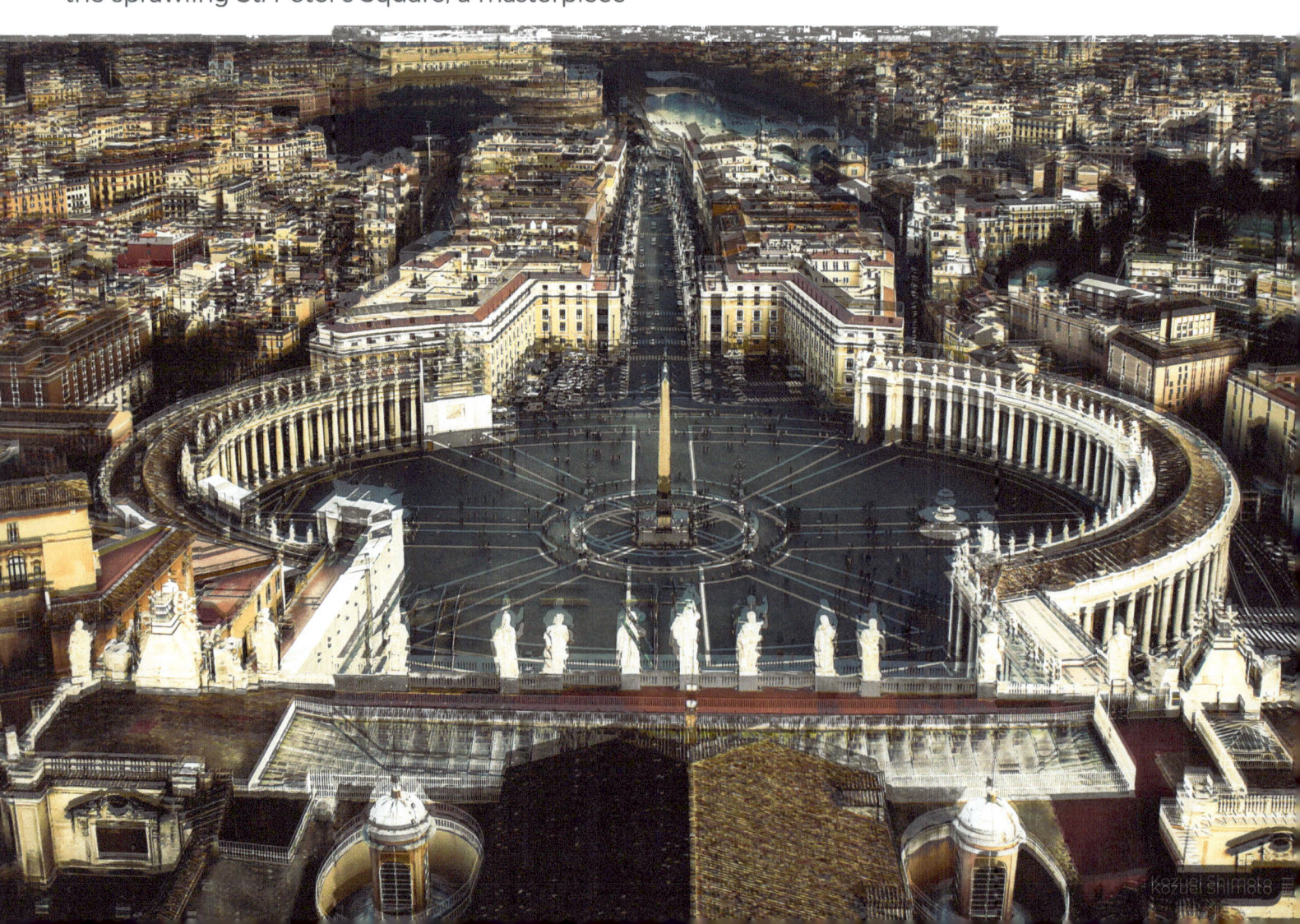

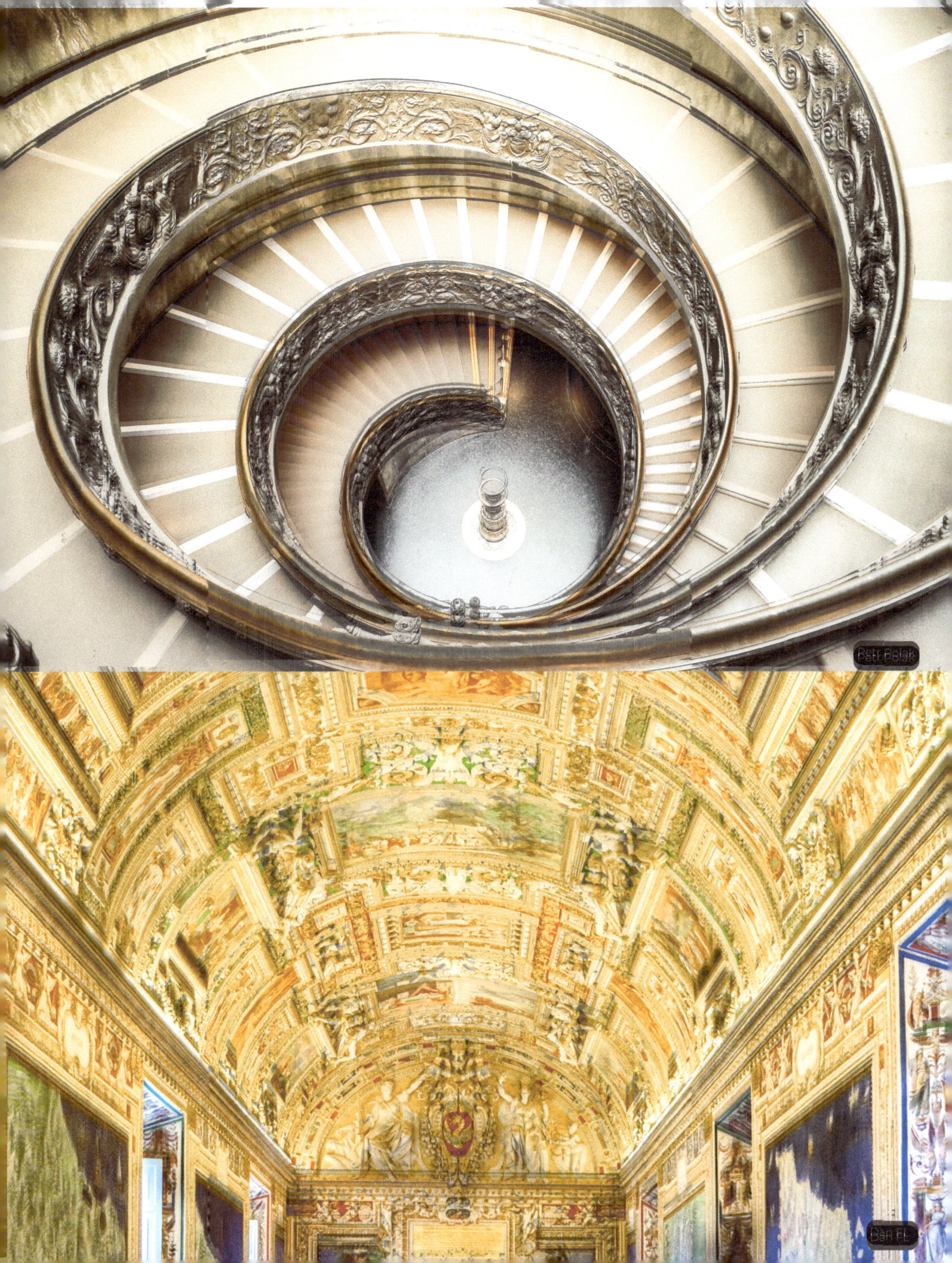

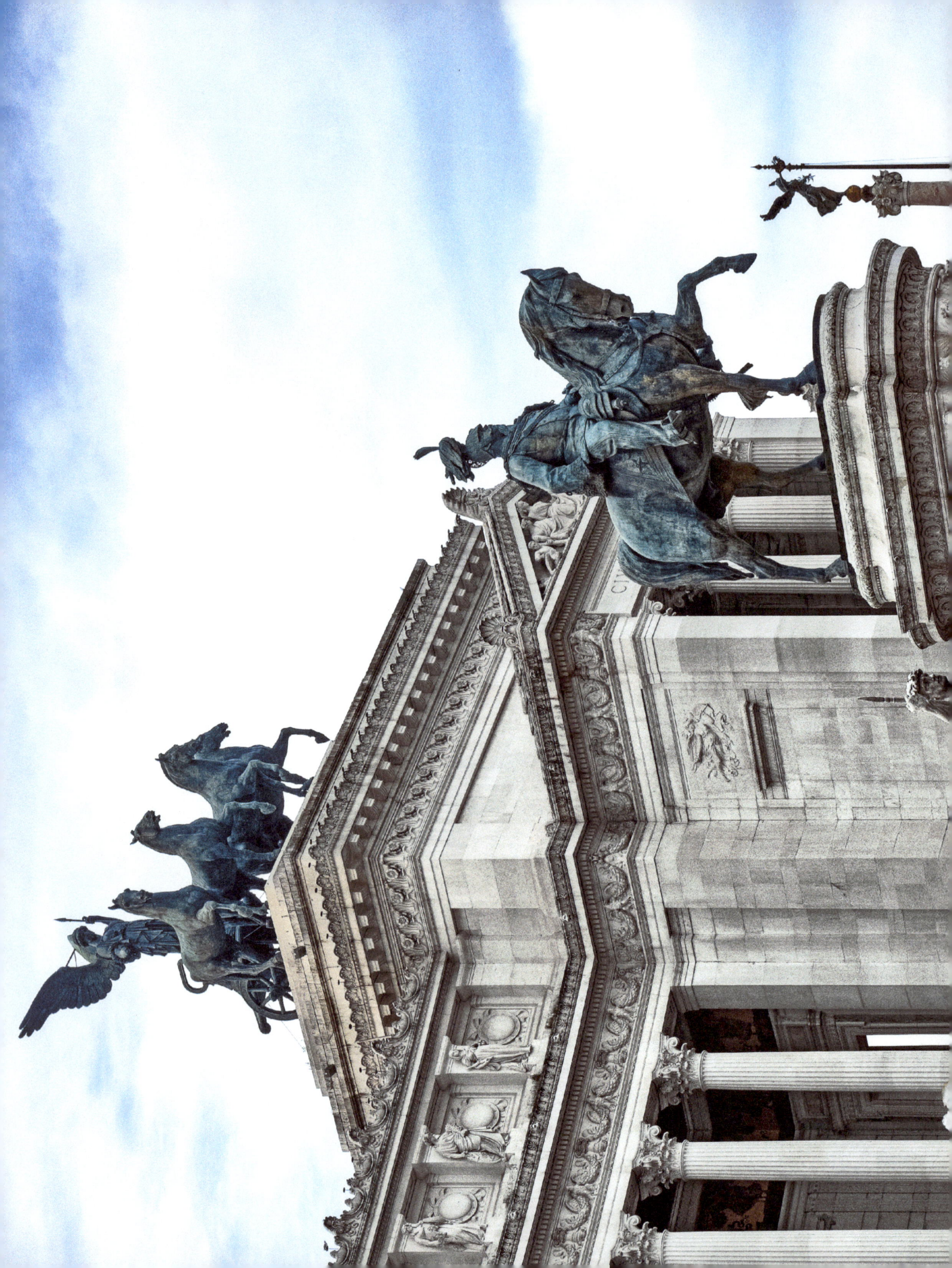

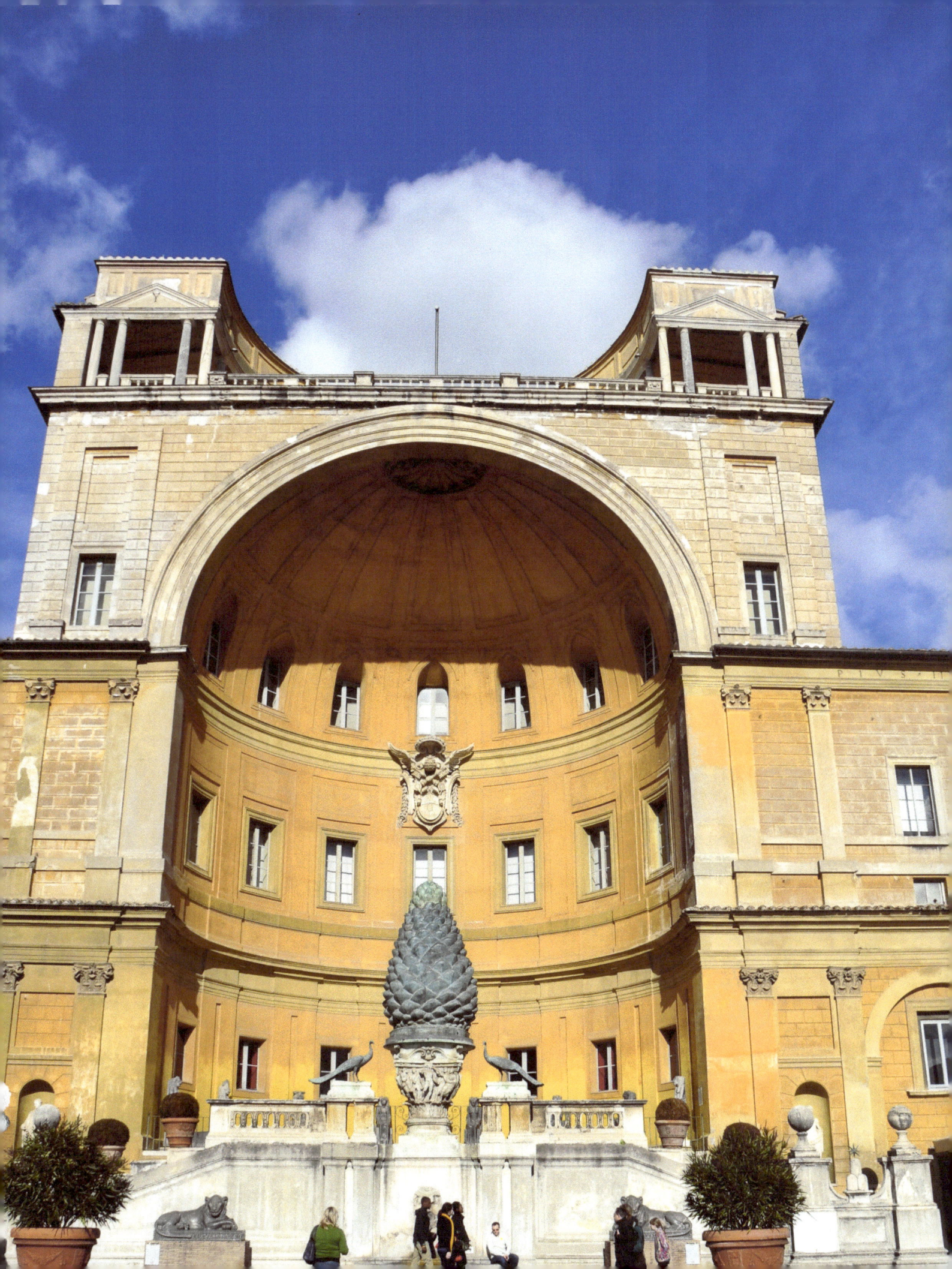

Piazza Navona

Piazza Navona, one of Rome's most picturesque squares, is a showcase of baroque artistry and lively urban culture. Once the site of ancient athletic contests, today it stands as a vibrant testament to the city's architectural and artistic heritage. The elongated shape of the piazza, following the outlines of the Stadium of Domitian that once stood here, creates a unique and open space, inviting visitors to wander and admire its artistic offerings.

Dominating the piazza is the Fountain of the Four Rivers, a Bernini masterpiece, featuring a towering Egyptian obelisk and intricate sculptures representing four major rivers from different continents. This central fountain is a marvel of baroque sculpture, capturing the dynamism and grandeur of the natural world.

Flanked by ornate baroque buildings, Piazza Navona is alive with the pulse of Rome's café culture. The square's perimeter is lined with charming eateries and street artists, adding a contemporary layer to its historical backdrop. The Church of Sant'Agnese in Agone, with its striking façade, overlooks the piazza, adding a spiritual dimension to this bustling public space. Piazza Navona is not just a square but a living, breathing embodiment of Rome's enduring charm, where history, art, and modern life seamlessly intertwine, offering a quintessential Roman experience.

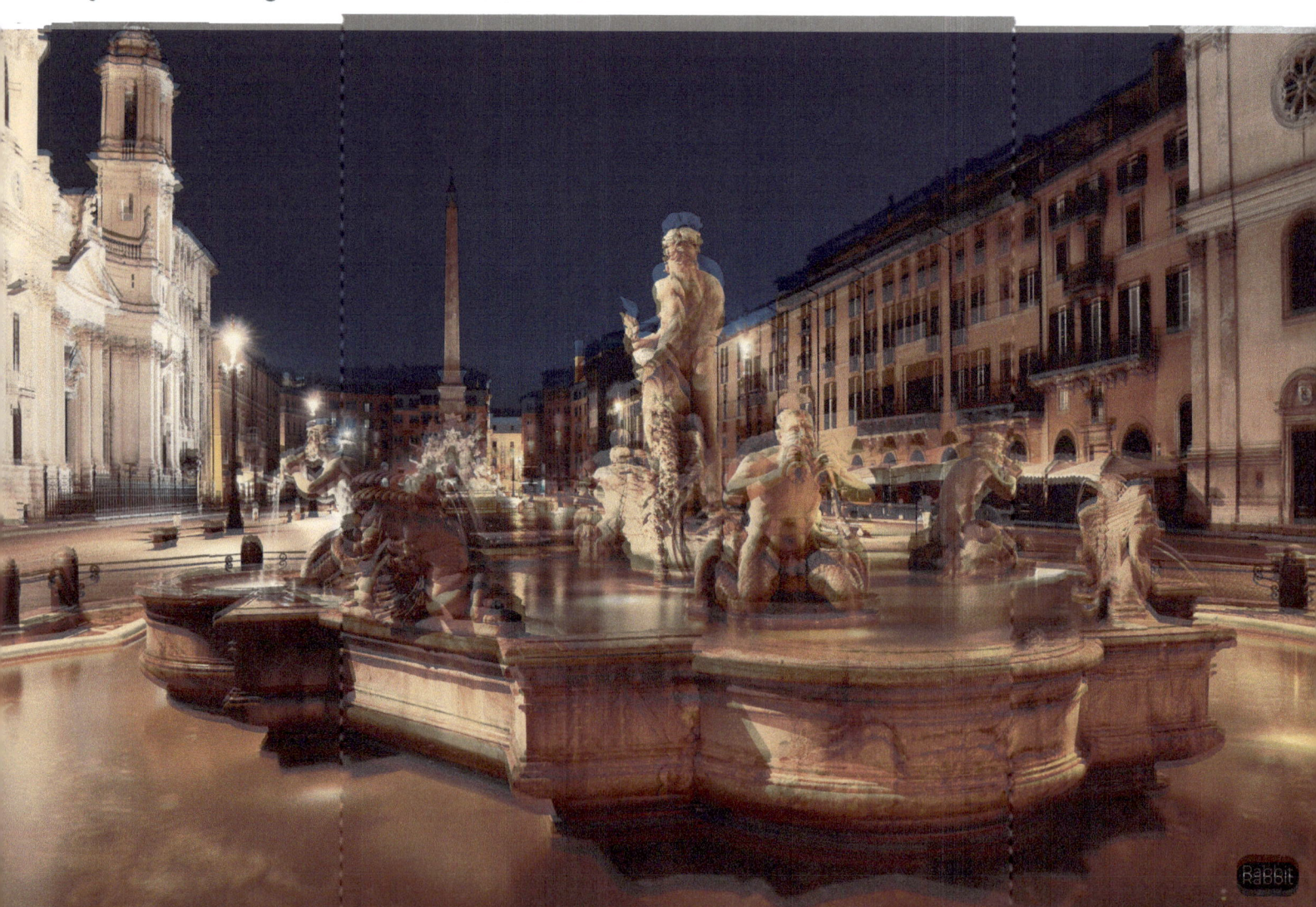

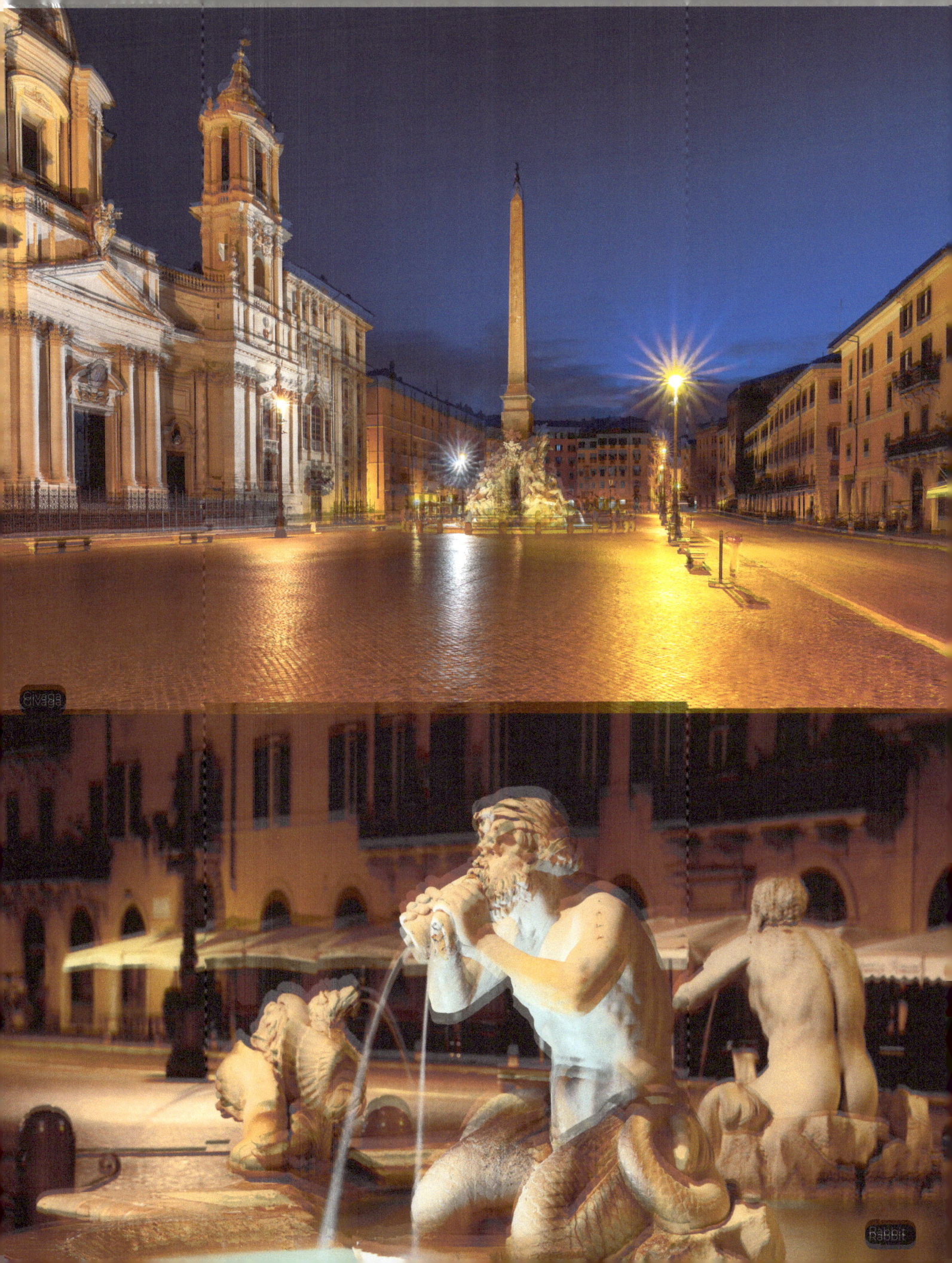

Trastevere

Trastevere, a charming district across the Tiber River, is the quintessence of Rome's enigmatic allure, blending a bohemian vibe with a rich historical tapestry. Known for its narrow, winding streets and medieval architecture, Trastevere feels like a step back in time, a world away from the grandeur of Rome's more famous landmarks.

The heart of Trastevere is its vibrant piazza, Piazza di Santa Maria, centered around the Basilica of Santa Maria in Trastevere, one of Rome's oldest churches. The basilica's glittering mosaics and time-worn façade offer a glimpse into the deep religious and artistic roots of the neighborhood. The streets around the piazza buzz with life, lined with trattorias, artisanal shops, and ivy-clad buildings, creating a picturesque tableau of Roman life.

Trastevere's charm lies in its authenticity; it's a district where daily life unfolds with an effortless grace. Locals and tourists alike are drawn to its lively bars and restaurants, where the spirit of Rome comes alive in the form of delicious cuisine and lively conversation. In the evenings, the cobblestone streets glow under the warm lights, and the air fills with music, making Trastevere not just a destination but an experience – a taste of the true, vibrant soul of Rome.

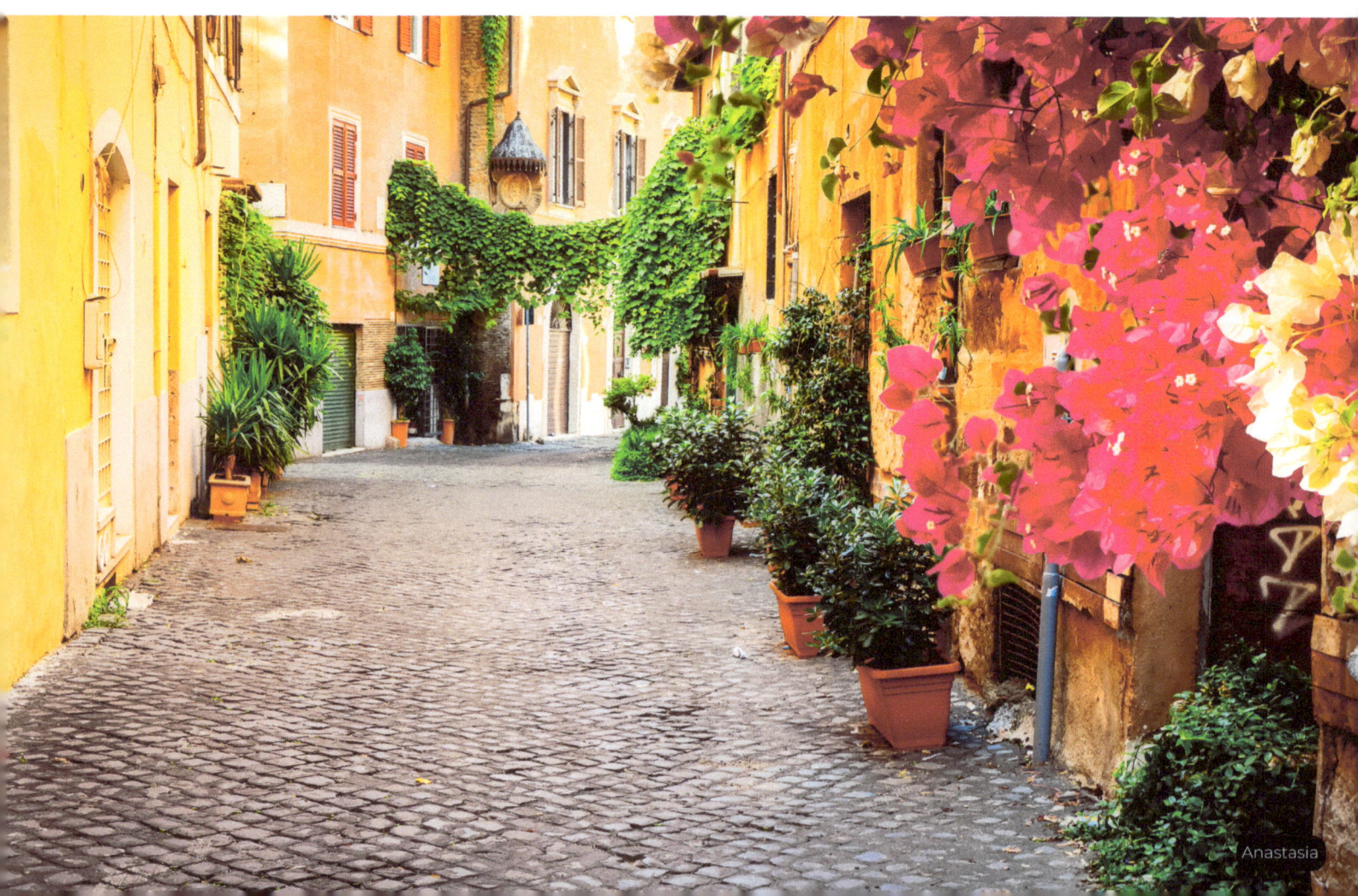

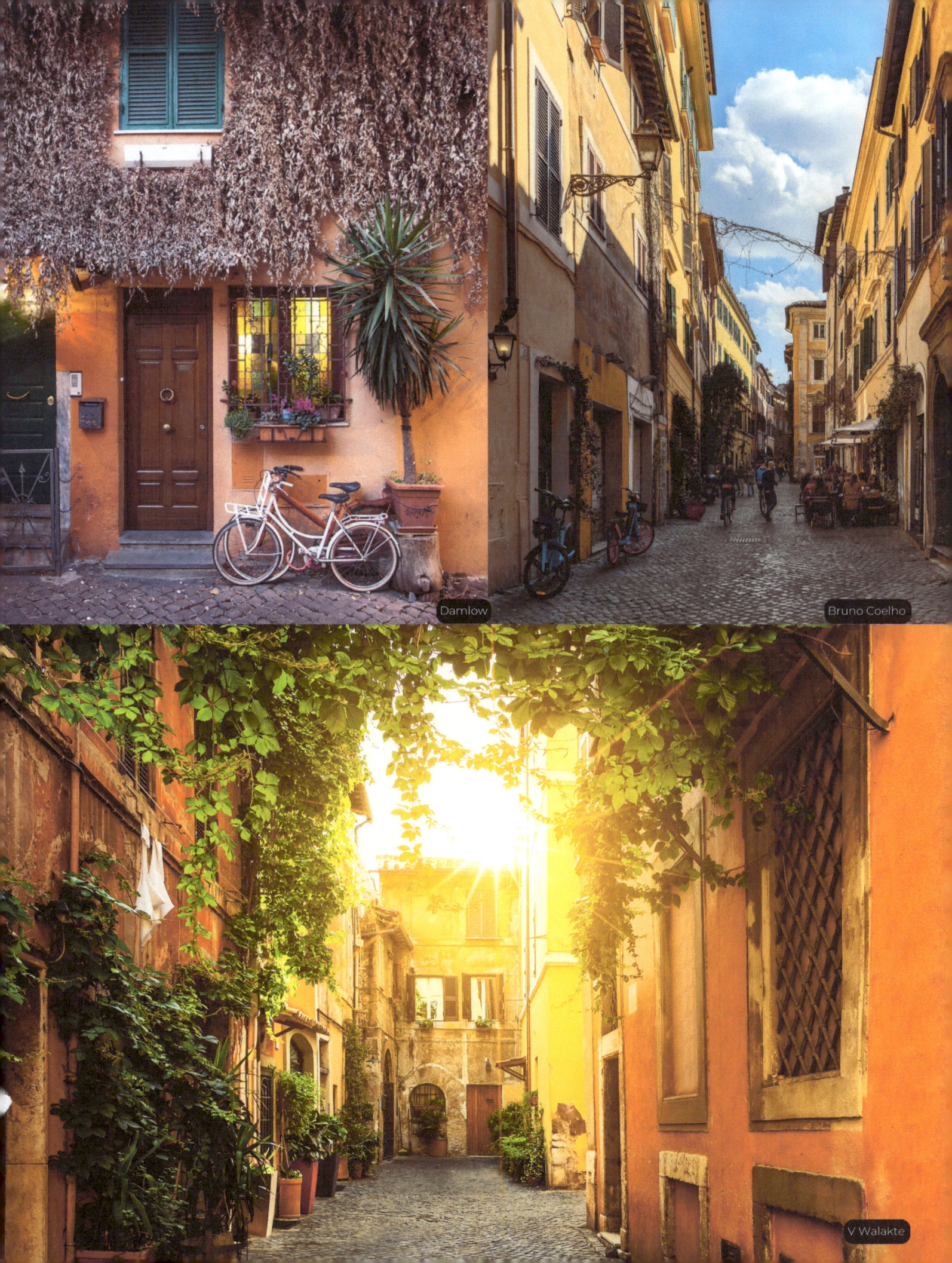

Basilica of Santa Maria Maggiore

The Basilica of Santa Maria Maggiore, resplendent on the Esquiline Hill, is one of Rome's four major basilicas and a monumental testament to religious art and history. This majestic church, dating back to the 5th century, is a blend of ancient and baroque architecture, encapsulating centuries of Christian heritage.

The façade, redesigned in the 18th century, leads to an interior of striking beauty. The basilica's nave retains its original stunning Ionic columns, while the triumphal arch and the apse are adorned with magnificent mosaics from the 5th century, depicting scenes from the Old Testament. These ancient mosaics, among the oldest in Christian art, resonate with the stories and teachings of early Christianity.

One of the basilica's most revered treasures is the Crypt of the Nativity, home to a relic of the Holy Crib. The coffered ceiling, gilded with the first gold brought from the New World, and the Sistine Chapel, not to be confused with its Vatican namesake, add to the church's artistic wealth.

Santa Maria Maggiore is not merely a place of worship but a repository of art and history. Its sacred and cultural significance is deeply interwoven with the fabric of Rome, offering visitors a profound experience of beauty, spirituality, and historical continuity.

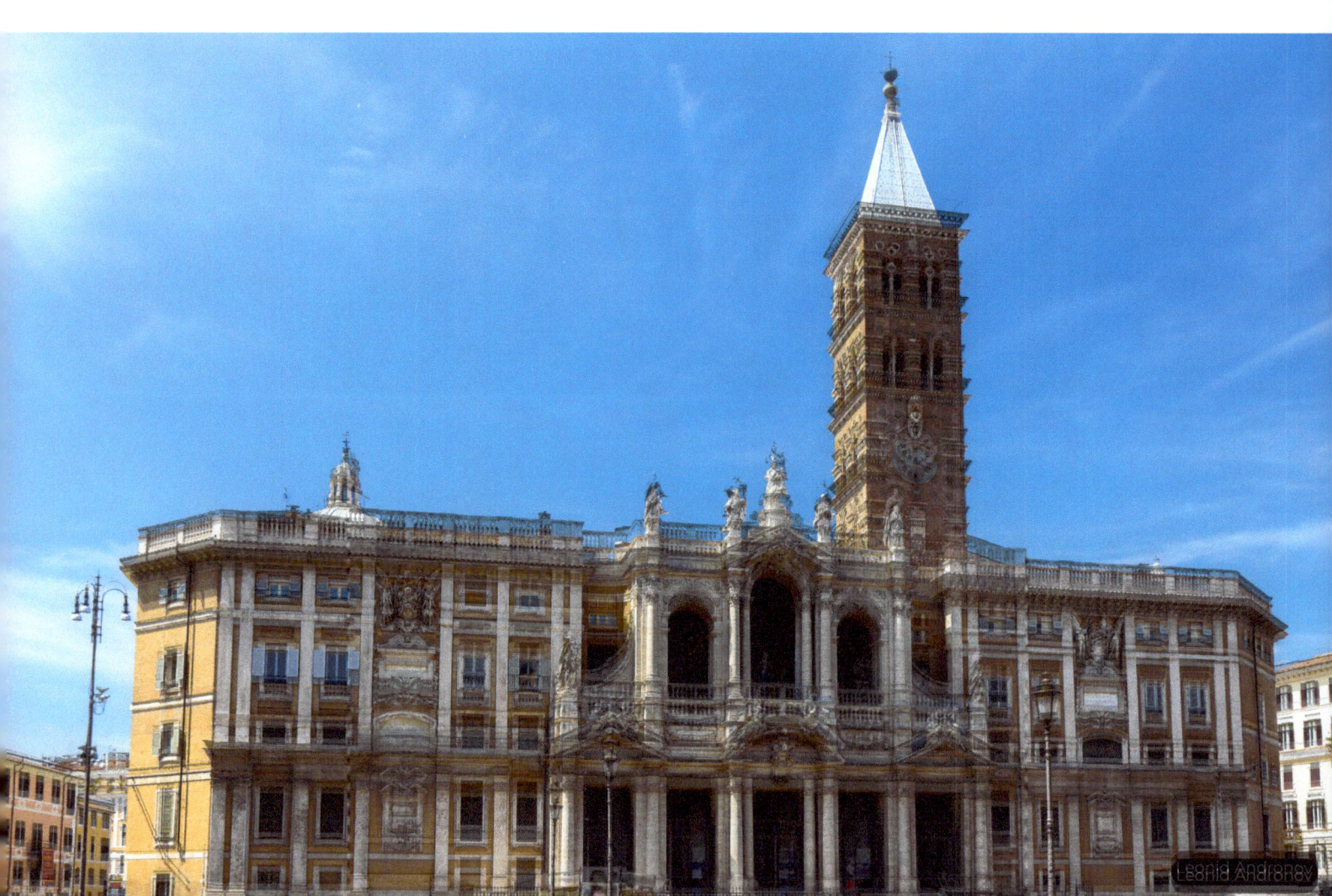

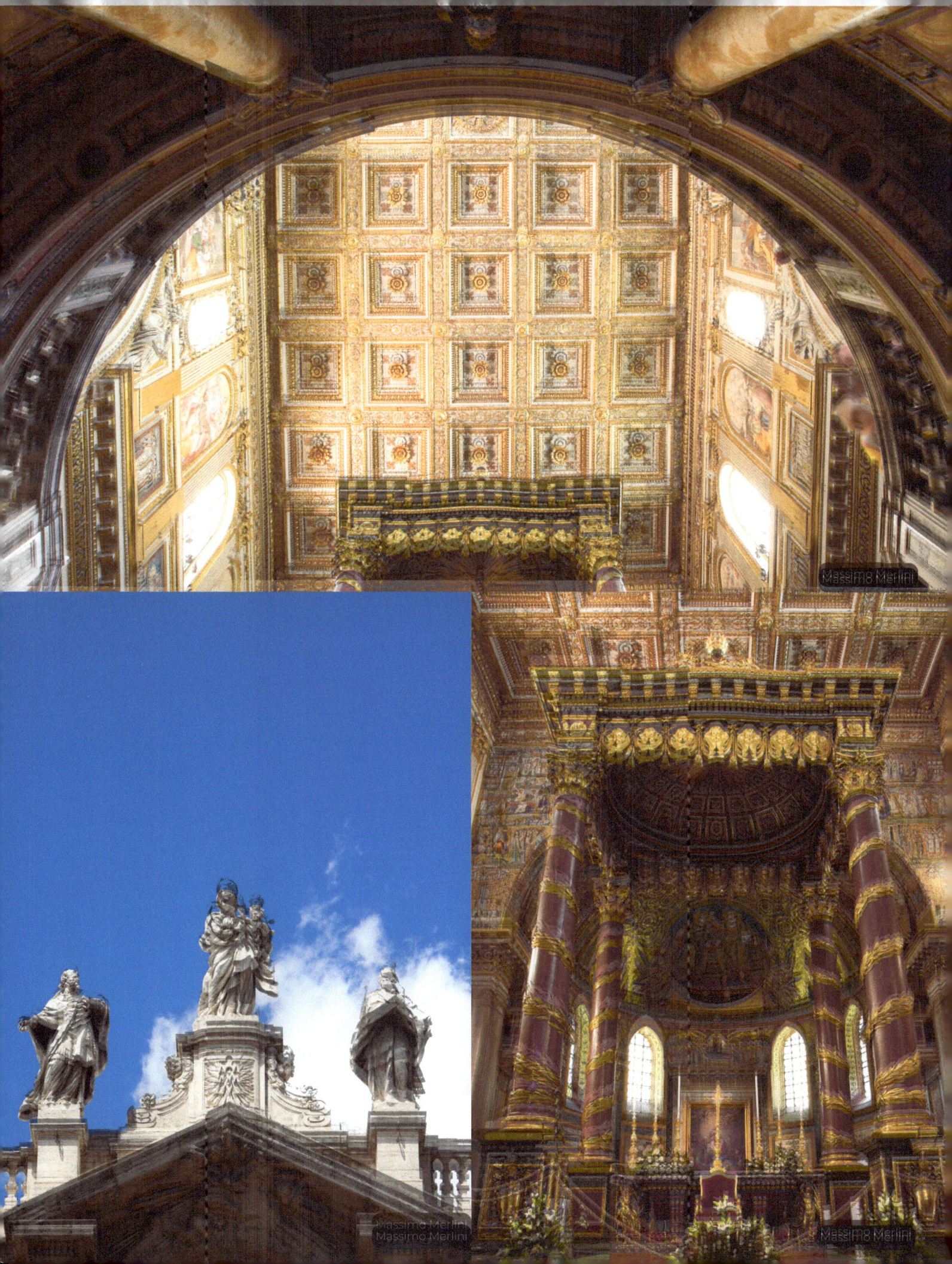

In "Discovering Rome - The Eternal City Pictorial," we journeyed through Rome's timeless beauty, from the majesty of the Colosseum to the spiritual serenity of Vatican City. Each page was a window into the soul of Rome, capturing its art, history, and vibrant culture. For those enchanted by this pictorial narrative and eager to delve deeper, "UNVEILING ROME - Your Travel Guide to The Eternal City" awaits. This comprehensive guide is your key to uncovering Rome's hidden gems and lesser-known attractions. Embark on a journey beyond the pages, where new beauty and unforgettable experiences in the Eternal City await your discovery.

UNVEILING ROME

Your Travel Guide to The Eternal City

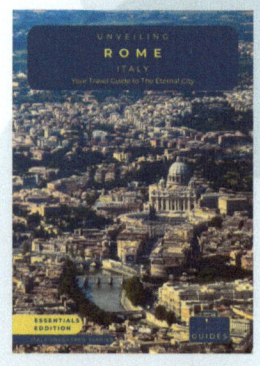

CHECK OUT THE FRANCE UNVEILED TRAVEL GUIDES SERIES

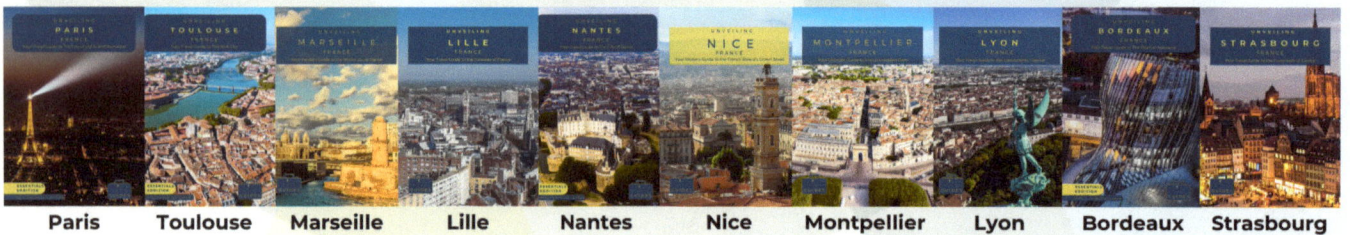

Paris | Toulouse | Marseille | Lille | Nantes | Nice | Montpellier | Lyon | Bordeaux | Strasbourg

CHECK OUT THE ITALY UNCOVERED TRAVEL GUIDES SERIES

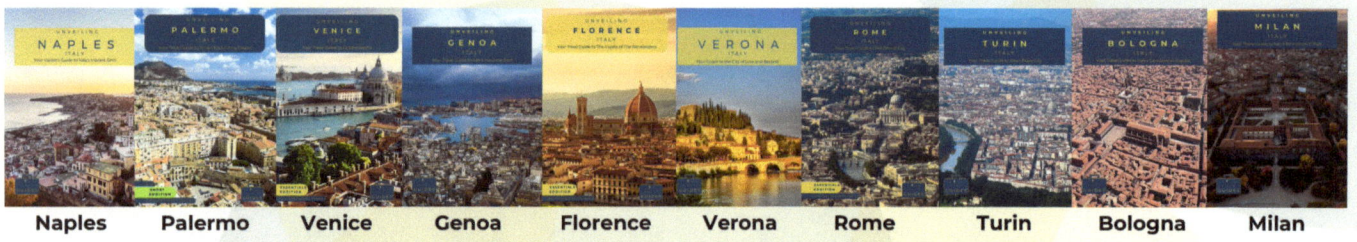

Naples | Palermo | Venice | Genoa | Florence | Verona | Rome | Turin | Bologna | Milan

CHECK OUT THE SPAIN UNVEILED TRAVEL GUIDES SERIES

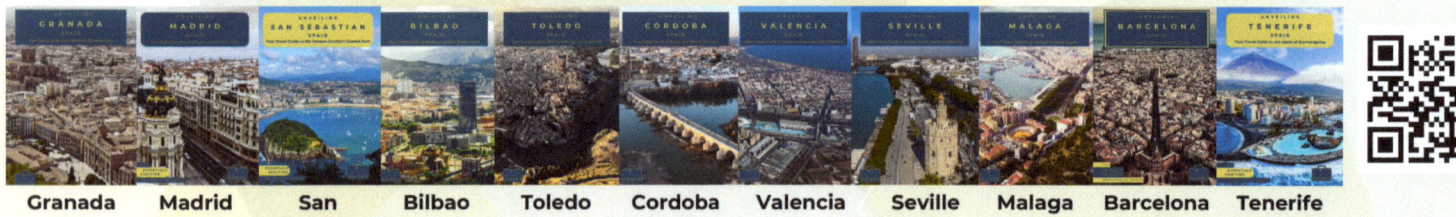

Granada | Madrid | San Sebastian | Bilbao | Toledo | Cordoba | Valencia | Seville | Malaga | Barcelona | Tenerife

Join our Tailored Travel Guides Network for more benefits by accessing this link:
https://mailchi.mp/d151cba349e8/ttgnetwork
Or by scanning the QR code

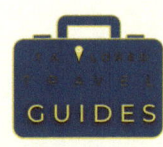

Discover your journey!

www.ingramcontent.com/pod-product-compliance
Lightning Source LLC
Chambersburg PA
CBHW051933210526
45473CB00006B/2230